The Case for Socialism

Alan Maass

CHICAGO, ILLINOIS

The Case for Socialism by Alan Maass

First published in 2001 as *Why You Should Be a Socialist*
by the International Socialist Organization

This updated edition published by Haymarket Books

ISBN 1-931859-09-4

Cover design by Ragina Johnson
Cover photo: Yale University workers' strike, September 2003
Cover photo by Michael Melillo

Haymarket Books
PO Box 180165, Chicago, IL 60618
www.haymarketbooks.org

Printed in Canada

2 4 6 8 10 9 7 5 3

Contents

Introduction

The United States is the land of freedom, prosperity, and opportunity, we're told. Ruth Schumacher must have her doubts.

Ruth gets up before the sun most mornings to get to her job, tending the breakfast bar at the Holiday Inn in Celina, a town of ten thousand in western Ohio near the border with Indiana. The 64-year-old great-grandmother makes all of $7 an hour for part-time work. She says she'd like to put out a tip jar, but management won't allow it.

Ruth and her husband Bob are getting by—barely. Bob earns $9 an hour as a janitor, but it's only part-time. The two draw $518 a month from their pension savings, but the premium on their health insurance plan eats up half of that.

After a lifetime of work, the Schumachers have to stretch every dollar. As for a retirement where they can enjoy their "golden years"—well, that's a dream deferred, thanks to Huffy Corporation.

Ten years ago, both Schumachers worked at the Huffy factory in Celina, the flagship plant for the country's leading maker of bicycles. The jobs at Huffy were good jobs—union jobs that paid a wage you could raise a family on, with decent benefits. The factory was the largest employer in town and the pride of Celina, which celebrated the company's famous fireball-red kids' bikes with parades and named its little-league baseball field Huffy Park.

That was then. In the mid-1990s, management declared that the company was getting beaten by overseas competition—and demanded a 30 percent pay cut. The Celina workers agreed. But it wasn't enough—in 1998, Huffy was back for more cuts. When the union wouldn't concede again, the company moved fast. Workers remember being called without warning to a meeting in the warehouse. Management said that they were closing the doors—and then got out of town quick, with a police escort.

Nearly one thousand workers were out of a job. Meanwhile, Huffy CEO Don Graber graciously accepted an increase in his annual salary and bonus to $1.1 million—to go along with $1.7 million in stock options. Graber's compensation in 1998 could have paid a full year's wage for one in eight workers laid off from the Celina plant.

These days, when Ruth leaves work at the Holiday Inn, she sometimes walks next door to the Wal-Mart—where she can find some good bargains, as she told a Gannett News Service reporter. Yet Wal-Mart is a big part of the reason why she lost her old job. Back in the 1990s, the superstore chain issued an ultimatum to the bosses at Huffy—sell their bikes for less, or else. That's when management decided that the union workforce at Celina would have to go.

Huffy first moved production to its nonunion plant in Farmington, Missouri, where workers made $8 an hour.

That didn't last long. After raking in more than $25 million in grants, low-interest loans, and other subsidies—given by the local community in return for the promise of new jobs—Huffy closed up shop in Farmington in 1999, and moved production overseas to factories in Mexico and China.

Eventually, Huffy decided that its Mexican workforce was costing too much, too. The company moved all its production to a factory near Beijing that the National Labor Committee, a corporate watchdog group, has identified as an appalling sweatshop. The Chinese workers who make Huffy bikes work seven days a week for thirteen to fifteen hours a day—for a wage that totals less than $20 a week. The company provides two meals a day—and the dormitories where workers sleep, packed twelve each into dank, cramped rooms.

So this "race to the bottom" that began with union jobs in western Ohio ends up in China, at a sweatshop where workers get less than 50 cents an hour. The Chinese workers aren't guilty of "stealing American jobs"—any more than the Huffy workers in Missouri should be accused of "stealing Ohio jobs." All are victims of a corporation consumed with finding cheaper labor—getting workers to work harder for less—no matter what the human cost.

Huffy may have gone farther and faster than other corporations, but it isn't the only one in the race. The victims of Corporate America's hunger for profits live in every corner of the world today—in the sweatshops and shantytowns of poor nations, and in the industrial cities of the richest countries.

"I've got a ground-zero plan," says Russell Luepnitz, who lost his job as a tool-and-die maker in Manitowoc, Wisconsin, in October 2003—one month shy of his sixtieth birthday. His wife Susan has gone back to work—even though she has Parkinson's disease. "If I don't get anything in six months, my unemployment runs out," Russell told the *Los Angeles Times*. "We'll have to sell our house and get an apartment. As my wife's health keeps backing off, she won't be able to keep working. We'll have to keep cutting back and cutting back, moving down the food chain so we can survive."

That's a reality that millions upon millions of people understand in today's America. But for the lucky few at the top of the "food chain," it's a different world.

People like Larry Ellison.

Ellison is the superrich CEO of the giant software corporation Oracle. He cofounded the company as a small consulting firm, and it grew from there—not because he had any special computer skills, but because he latched onto an idea for business software developed by other people and started selling it before anyone else. Ellison became a millionaire, then a billionaire, then a multibillionaire.

Today, there is no luxury that he can't afford, no interest that he can't pursue, no door closed to him. He owns a yacht, of course—one that's nearly as long as a football field. There's the private plane and a fleet of fancy cars. But topping all of it is Ellison's new villa, under construction for years in the exclusive town of Woodside, California.

Ellison's "home" will cost more than $100 million. The enormous main building, five guest houses, and assorted other structures—including three garages for Ellison's fourteen cars—are designed to look like a sixteenth-century Japanese village. The grounds are covered with a literal forest of Japanese trees, interspersed with ponds and streams, hills, and a 2.7-acre lake fed by two waterfalls.

The lake is filled with purified drinking water.

Luxury on this scale is hard to grasp—like the stories about France's Louis XVI and Marie Antoinette. But what is even more incredible is the fact that all this is small potatoes for Larry Ellison. In 2003, according to *Forbes* magazine, he was the sixth-richest person in the world, worth $16.6 billion. That means he could afford to build ninety-nine more palatial estates, each with a price tag of $100 million, and still remain a multibillionaire.

Larry Ellison is worth more today—a lot more—than the one thousand workers laid off by Huffy in Celina, Ohio, made in wages in all their years working at the bicycle factory, some of them for half a lifetime.

These are two different worlds. Larry Ellison lives in one, a world of privilege and power where he can indulge any whim.

Ruth Schumacher and Russell Luepnitz—like the vast majority of people in the United States and around the globe—belong to a different world. It's a world of poverty and despair for large numbers—whether they're suffering through tough times after being laid off, or they were *born* into tough times and never had a shot at anything else. For the many others who have steady jobs and can keep their heads above water, they nevertheless have to struggle every day to make ends meet.

Look beyond the borders of the United States, and this tale of two worlds is even more extreme. Some 1.2 billion people around the world survive on less than $1 a day—and almost one-half of the global population lives on $2 a day or less, according to the *Human Development Report* produced by the United Nations. Meanwhile, the total wealth of the three richest families in the world is equal to the combined economic output of the world's forty-eight least developed countries.

What could possibly explain this incredible gap—between the pampered and privileged lives of a tiny few and the poverty endured by billions of people around the world?

The most important thing to understand is that it isn't an accident.

It isn't simply that some people in the world are rich and some people are poor. The truth is that some people in the world are rich *because* other people are poor. People like Larry Ellison are rich *because* people like Ruth Schumacher have been driven all their lives to work harder for less—until they're kicked aside. Some people are rich *because* others go hungry, *because* others have nowhere to live, *because* others endure the horrors of war, *because* the future of the environment is put in jeopardy.

That is the ugly truth about the capitalist society we live in. And Larry Ellison doesn't even try to hide it. He's known for paraphrasing the thirteenth-century warlord Genghis Khan: "It's not enough that we win; everyone else must lose."

This perfectly sums up Ellison's business methods. In 2003, he and Oracle carried out a hostile takeover bid for a rival software company called PeopleSoft. Their openly expressed purpose was to wreck PeopleSoft—eliminate products that might compete with Oracle's, fire thousands of employees, steal the top programmers.

This kind of ruthlessness is the rule in Corporate America. Thus, as the U.S. economy began slumping in 2000,

CEOs at major companies that announced layoffs of one thousand or more workers received almost twice as much in pay and bonuses as the average CEO, according to *Business Week* magazine's annual review. "CEOs who want to keep their jobs must be willing to cut others' when earnings decline," chirped the *Denver Post* in April 2001. "They must take money away from the people who built the company, and give it to the people who financed it."

Steal from the workers...and give to the bankers, the bosses, and the Wall Street speculators. Karl Marx couldn't have put it more clearly.

The priorities of capitalism certainly don't stop at the borders of the United States—as the U.S. government is proving in Iraq.

George W. Bush and his fellow Texas oilmen in the White House used a variety of cover stories to justify their war, but the real aim was clear from the opening days of the invasion, when the first priority for U.S. and British forces was to protect the oilfields. Likewise, when U.S. troops rolled into Baghdad, setting off chaos and looting, there was one Iraqi government building where marines stood guard—the Ministry of Oil.

And who has paid the price? More than one million Iraqis are dead because of more than a decade of U.S. military and economic warfare. One U.S. official unintentionally revealed the truth in a comment to a reporter about whether Iraqi families whose loved ones had been killed by U.S. forces would be paid compensation. "How much is a life worth?" the official said. "The value of a life in Iraq is probably a lot less than it would be in the U.S. or Britain."

What a sick comment about the world we live in—that some bureaucrat in Washington would dare to calculate the lesser value of an Iraqi life. But the truth is that this is entirely in keeping with the logic of an economic and political system that puts profits and power before human need.

There is an alternative—socialism.

Socialism is based on a few simple and straightforward principles. The world's vast resources should be used not to increase the wealth of a few parasites, but to eradicate poverty and homelessness and every other form of scarcity forever. Rather than fighting wars that promote the power of the tiny class of rulers at the top, the working majority in society should cooperate in the project of creating a world of plenty. The important decisions shouldn't be left in the hands of people who are either rich or are controlled by people who are rich, but should be made by everyone democratically. Instead of a system that crushes our hopes and dreams, we should live in a world where we control our own lives.

These socialist principles have been part of a rich tradition of struggle against inequality and injustice—a struggle that is more relevant today than ever.

The corporate-run media would have us believe that opposition to the status quo is "utopian" and "out of style." But all their cheerleading for war couldn't stop a massive outpouring of opposition to George W. Bush's invasion of Iraq. Tens of millions of people around the world marched against the war—and their protests spoke for the doubts and questions of countless others. Even the pro-war *New York Times* had to observe: "The fracturing of the Western alliance over Iraq and the huge antiwar demonstrations around the world this week-end are reminders that there may still be two superpowers on the planet: the United States and world public opinion."

The hope for an alternative to the rotten world we see around us lies with mobilizing such struggles—against war and militarism, and all the countless other protests against a system that breeds violence and poverty and environmental destruction.

According to the United Nations Development Program, the cost of providing the most basic needs that go unmet around the world—for food, shelter, clean water, primary education, basic medical care—would be just $80 billion a year. The three richest men in America—Bill Gates, Warren Buffett, and Paul Allen—could have covered this cost in 2003 with plenty to spare. The U.S. government spends five times more than that every year on the military.

Can there possibly be a good reason why the world's poor aren't lifted out of poverty? If Bill Gates's billions or a small portion of the Pentagon's budget could abolish hunger and disease right now, then what kind of a society would refuse to take the steps necessary to end the suffering?

It is a society that needs to be replaced—by socialism. The goal of this book is to show why—and how.

CHAPTER ONE

American Dream or American Nightmare?

Will your children live a better life than you?

For three decades following the Second World War, most people in the United States could answer "yes." That answer was the basis of what was known as the "American Dream"—the belief that working people, and not just the rich, could look forward to a steadily increasing standard of living and a better future for themselves and their children. Wages grew—not spectacularly, but enough so that most families could afford more. Millions of young people became the first in their families to go to college. Diseases that had plagued society for centuries were conquered.

The American Dream was modest. It didn't change the fact that the Rockefellers and the Gettys led much better lives than anyone else, thanks only to the fact that they were born into wealth. And the dream didn't include everyone. In particular, African Americans remained second-class citizens, especially under the apartheid system of the Jim Crow South.

But for a majority of people in the United States, the system of capitalism seemed to produce, if not spectacular wealth, then at least new benefits unknown to previous generations. Most people could hope to enjoy a better life as the years went by.

Today, the American Dream is dead. For twenty-five years, the majority of people in the United States have seen their living standards grow worse, not better. Wages for most of the population have stagnated or fallen. Getting through college has become a huge financial burden. People who had been confident that their livelihoods were secure found out that they weren't—and those who haven't lost their jobs are working longer and harder.

Rather than confidence about the present and hope for the future, working people in the U.S. today worry about holding on to what we have—and fear that the future will be even less secure.

Working harder...or hardly working

As the Christmas holiday approached in 2002, George Bush showed up for a photo op at the Capitol Area Food Bank in Washington, D.C. "I hope people around this country realize that agencies such as this food bank need money," Bush scolded for the TV cameras. "Contributions are down. They shouldn't be down in a time of need."

This from the man whose own inaction a few weeks earlier became the cause for large numbers of people to turn to food banks to feed their families. Bush's administration sat on its hands as Congress adjourned before taking up legislation to extend emergency federal unemployment benefits. So right after Christmas, nearly one million people got a special present from Washington. They were cut off.

Through most of 2003, the number of people officially counted as unemployed in the U.S. hovered at more than eight million—about 6 percent of the labor force, a relatively low jobless rate compared to previous recessions. But there's a lot that you couldn't tell from the official statistics.

Nearly one in five people in the United States was laid off at some point during the three years following the turn of the decade. Among people with incomes below $40,000 a year—roughly speaking, the poorer two-thirds of the population—it was closer to one in four who got the ax.

The 2001 recession and the years of economic slump that followed were much more serious for large numbers of workers than the statistics showed. For one thing, the official unemployment rate doesn't include the large and growing number of "discouraged workers" who have given up on finding a job at all. Another hidden group is people forced to take part-time work because they can't find full-time employment—nearly five million people as of the end of 2003. Put these categories together, and the true rate of underemployment was twice as high as the official figure.

But even a more accurate calculation misses the full story. The first jobs to go in the recession were quality jobs in manufacturing that paid relatively well and provided decent benefits—thanks, usually, to the higher rate of unionization for blue-collar work. Factory employment in the U.S. peaked in 1979 at around twenty million workers. Since then, one in four of these jobs has disappeared. It took twenty years for the first 2.5 million to go. The second 2.5 million—and then some—vanished in the first three years of the Bush administration.

The first thing that these millions of laid-off workers learned is that they couldn't expect to find jobs that would pay as well as their old ones—when they could find work at all. By the end of 2003, wages in industries that were adding jobs were more than 20 percent lower than industries where employment was declining, according to an analysis by the Economic Policy Institute.

Those who survived the layoff ax didn't have much to celebrate, either. Corporate America responded to falling profits as the recession took hold by looking for every way to squeeze workers. In particular, union members faced relentless pressure from employers determined not just to keep wages in check and reduce benefits, but to undermine work rules built up over years of struggle.

One favorite tactic of the employers is called outsourcing—shifting work away from better-paid union members to nonunion subcontractors. Thus, in 2002, the telecommunications equipment maker Lucent Technologies claimed poverty when it slashed nearly one thousand union jobs at its North Andover, Massachussetts, factory. But even as it was sending out pink slips, Lucent hired a labor contractor, Solectron, to fill the newly opened positions—inside the *same* factory. Masking tape on the floor of the plant marked the dividing line for union and nonunion workers.

The ongoing destruction of the kind of decent-paying jobs that gave workers the hope that they and their families would enjoy a better way of life didn't begin with the Bush years. This was a theme even in the "best of times"—the long economic expansion during the 1990s.

To the corporate media, this was the "miracle economy."

Yet in 1998, as the boom was reaching the high point in the longest period of uninterrupted economic growth since records were kept, corporate layoffs hit the highest level in a decade—higher even than the recession years of the early 1990s, according to the Challenger, Gray & Christmas consulting firm. As the *Minneapolis Star Tribune* put it: "Layoffs used to be a sign of bad times in Corporate America. These days, job cuts are a signal that good times aren't good enough."

Bill Clinton and the Democrats never tire of boasting about the millions of new jobs created during the 1990s. But according to a study by the Jobs with Justice union coalition, 74 percent of the jobs that grew fastest in the 1990s paid less than a living wage—and 46 percent paid less than half a living wage. In the midst of the "miracle" economy, it was possible to work two and even three of these "McJobs"—and still not earn enough to lift a family out of poverty.

No wonder the fastest-growing part of the workforce is the "working poor." Such a concept didn't exist a generation ago—the ranks of the poor were invariably the unfortunate few who couldn't find work. No longer. As of 2002, two-thirds of families with children whose household incomes were below the official poverty line had at least one family member who worked, often year-round and more than forty hours a week.

Even for those above the poverty line, it's a scramble for working families to make ends meet. If you strip away the media impressionism about consumer spending and Internet revolutions—and take account of the growing costs of a variety of necessities, especially health care and child care—it's clear that working people are having a harder time today around most of the issues at the core of their lives.

Between 1979 and 2002, income for the median U.S. household—that is, families at the middle of the income ladder—rose very slowly, at an average of less than 1 percent a year, after adjusting for inflation. But even this isn't the whole story. The tiny increase is entirely the result of households working harder and longer. According to the Economic Policy Institute's *State of Working America, 2002/2003*, the average middle-income, two-parent family works 660 more hours a year than in 1979. That's an additional sixteen weeks' worth of full-time employment, just to keep living standards from going backward.

It reminds you of what the Red Queen told Alice in Lewis Carroll's *Through the Looking-Glass*: "Here, you see, it takes all the running you can do to keep in the same place. If you want to get somewhere else, you must run at least twice as fast as that!"

There's no doubt about where the money went, either. During the same period from 1979 to 2002, when median household income essentially stagnated, the income of the richest 1 percent of the U.S. population more than tripled.

The 1980s was known as the "decade of greed" because of the huge transfer of wealth from the poorest to the richest in the United States. But it turns out that the greed was just beginning. By 2000, before-tax income was more heavily concentrated at the very top of the income ladder than at any time since 1929—on the eve of the Great Depression.

"No country without a revolution or a military defeat and subsequent occupation has ever experienced such a sharp shift in the distribution of earnings as America has in the last generation," economist Lester Thurow summarized at the midpoint of the 1990s. Since then, inequality in the United States. has only grown more pronounced.

These facts barely register in a mainstream media addicted to telling only good news about the U.S. economy. But they are very much a part of the lives led by the working majority in U.S. society. And they've contributed to a deep pool of bitterness and anger. The truth is that the American Dream exists only for the handful of people at the top who've become fantastically rich at our expense. For everyone else, the American Dream is dead.

Sickness of the health care system

Income and wealth aren't the only ways to measure the deteriorating quality of life for working people. Consider, for example, what happens when we get sick.

In terms of technology and resources, the U.S. has the most advanced health care system in the world. Yet health care is a chronic source of fear and uncertainty for those lucky enough to remain healthy—and a nightmare for those who get sick.

Ask Rose Shaffer. At sixty, she suffered a heart attack that nearly killed her—would have killed her, if she hadn't been rushed to an emergency room near her home in the south suburbs of Chicago. But three years afterward, she feels as if the hospital is trying to steal back the life it saved, as she put it to a reporter from Britain's *Guardian* newspaper.

Rose was uninsured, and the hospital owners—Advocate Heath Care, a giant hospital chain that claims to be Christian and not for profit—hounded her relentlessly for a bill totaling tens of thousands of dollars. Rose says that Advocate sent debt collectors after her, who called at all hours of the day and night, at home and at work, until she finally declared bankruptcy. Now, at an age where she had hoped to be retired, Rose works seven days a week for a nursing agency in order to keep her modest house.

Some 43.6 million people in the United States were without health insurance in 2003—a number that has continued to grow as fewer and fewer companies provide health benefits to their employees. For one in every seven people in the U.S., the only thing that stands between them and destitution is an accident or serious illness.

The health care disaster also extends to those with insurance—as the Wooldridge family knows all too well. In October 1995, Glenn and Jamie Wooldridge lost their four-month-old daughter Elizabeth—officially, to complications from cystic fibrosis. But the Wooldridges blame their HMO, which repeatedly refused permission for doctors to perform a $128 "sweat test" to confirm the diagnosis.

Elizabeth's older sister Aereanna was later diagnosed with cystic fibrosis, too—so the Wooldridges' ordeal with the health care industry continues. They have faced a maze of paperwork and hoops to jump through at every step. "I can't describe it, I really can't," Jamie told the San Francisco television station KRON-TV. "You just do the same thing over and over again...That's the difference between then and now, but we didn't realize that at first with Elizabeth, and now we do. Until you're here, you think everything is fine. But when you're here, you realize how big of a hole you're in and how hard you have to fight to keep your children alive."

What a sick system that forces parents like Glenn and Jamie to "fight to keep their children alive." Yet horror stories like this one became commonplace as "managed care" came to dominate the industry over the course of the 1990s, providing health care to 93 percent of U.S. workers and retirees with insurance by 2001.

"Mangled care" was supposed to be the solution to rising health costs. HMOs would cut out the waste and keep an eye on doctors who ordered unnecessary tests and procedures, saving consumers big money. But it was the HMOs that made the big money—by restricting care. Their philosophy was summed up by Richard Rainwater, cofounder of the for-profit HMO Columbia/HCA: "The day has come when somebody has to do in the hospital business what McDonald's has done in the fast-food business and what Wal-Mart has done in the retailing business."

Ask almost anyone who's had contact with the health care non-system in this country, and they'll tell you that they're sick of it. That especially includes health care workers—even doctors—who have been under increasing pressure to cut corners on patient care. At many hospitals, short staffing is chronic—to the point that conditions become dangerous for patient and caregiver alike.

Poll after poll shows that a majority of Americans want a national health system that guarantees care for everyone. In fact, a *Wall Street Journal* survey found that more than half of those asked would be willing to pay $2,000 a year extra in taxes to guarantee health care for those who don't have access to it.

Yet Washington has only made the problem worse. Early in the 1990s, the Clinton administration came into office promising comprehensive health care reform. But rather than alienate the powerful health care bosses, Clinton bargained away one point after another until the effort collapsed. A decade later, George W. Bush made his own mark—with a so-called "reform" of the government-run Medicare health care system for the elderly that will further line the pockets of industry giants by increasing the already staggering financial burden on seniors.

What exists in the United States today is really two health care systems—one for the haves and one for the have-nots. For the rich, no expense is spared in using the latest techniques and technologies on medical problems. For the rest, health care is "rationed." Drugs and treatments that could help people live longer, healthier, and more fulfilling lives are often beyond reach because of a bewildering array of restrictions—imposed in the interests of the bottom line.

So it's no surprise that the most important factors determining a person's health have nothing to do with diet or exercise or smoking. The most important factors are social class and race.

The war on the poor

The American Dream never did exist for one group of Americans—the poor. And if life has become more difficult for all working people, it is a disaster for the growing numbers thrown on the trash heap in the richest country in the world.

As of 2002, 34.6 million people—about one in eight Americans—lived below the official poverty line, according to the U.S. Census Bureau. A survey by the U.S. Conference of Mayors found that requests for emergency food assistance jumped by nearly 20 percent in 2002. Requests for emergency shelter assistance grew by an average of 19 percent in the 18 cities that reported an increase, the fastest rise in a decade.

These are grim statistics. But by themselves, they don't capture the terrors of being poor in the United States. It's like walking through a minefield—where one false step can lead to catastrophe.

That's what happened to Janice Foster. In early 1998, she lost documents that she needed to remain on welfare. After her benefits were cut off, she fell behind on the rent, and in July of that year, she and her three children were evicted. She began the ordeal that occupies all the time and effort of so many of the poor—trying to arrange a place to live for short periods with friends or relatives, or in down-and-out hotels.

By August, she had failed. Janice and her children ended up at the Union Rescue Mission homeless shelter in the middle of Los Angeles' Skid Row—a human dumping ground on the edge of the city's downtown. There, in the shadow of fancy skyscrapers, three-year-old Deon, four-year-old Shayla, and their fourteen-year-old brother William played in the alleys—among men sleeping in cardboard boxes and using drugs in the doorways.

There are plenty of well-fed academics who claim to understand why people like Janice and her children have gone through hell. "If poor people behaved rationally, they would seldom be poor for long in the first place," sniffed New York University political science professor Lawrence Mead in an interview with author Jonathan Kozol.

Smug words. But among the millions of people with stories like Janice's, there is little "irrational" about anything they did. The only thing irrational is the miserable circumstances that they had to deal with in the first place. "If only I could, I would have done things differently," Janice told a *New York Times* reporter, thinking back on the events that landed her and her family on Skid Row. "I would have saved more money. But really, I didn't have any money to save."

Yet blaming the poor for being poor is at the heart of everything the politicians say and do about poverty.

In 2002, George Bush signed legislation that reauthorized the system for aid to the poor transformed by Bill Clinton's welfare "reform" law in 1996. Bush's contempt for the most vulnerable could be seen in two priorities of the religious right that showed up in the reauthorization bill—$300 million a year in spending to promote "healthy marriages," and an increase in the work requirement for recipients to keep their benefits.

Strangely, the Bush administration didn't feel the need to make gainful employment a requirement to receive the benefits of its $1.35 trillion tax cut giveaway, passed the year before—nearly half of which is going to the corporate tycoons, Wall Street speculators, and billionaire heirs who make up the richest 1 percent of the U.S. population.

But when it comes to welfare, Bush is only an accessory after the fact to the original crime—committed by Bill Clinton in 1996 when he adopted Republican proposals to "reform" the welfare system. Clinton's law abolished the federal government's main welfare program, Aid to Families with Dependent Children—and replaced it with a system full of new rules to punish the poor.

And it didn't stop there. The law slashed $54 billion over six years from all kinds of programs—from food stamps to Supplementary Security Income for disabled children. According to the Urban Institute, the poorest one-fifth of U.S. families lost an average of $1,310 a year in benefits of all sorts as a result of the 1996 law. More than $100 a month—that's the difference between hard times and destitution for millions of people.

Yet the consensus in Washington is that welfare "reform" is a success. Five years after Clinton signed the legislation, the welfare rolls had been cut in half—to about eight million people.

Success? The 1990s economic expansion may have hidden the consequences for a while, but numerous reports show that between a third and half of recipients who left the welfare rolls couldn't find regular work. The average wage for former recipients is less than $7 an hour. Two-thirds of those who got jobs didn't have health insurance coverage, and child care remained a chronic problem. According to one study at the end of the 1990s, about half of former recipients said that they had skipped a meal to make food last until the end of the month, and 40 percent said they haven't been able to pay rent, mortgage, or utility bills at least once in the previous year.

This isn't success. It's a disaster—suffered by the most vulnerable people in the world's richest country.

The politics of scapegoating

It was the kind of rhetoric that all politicians have come to use on Martin Luther King Jr.'s birthday. "[W]e renew our commitment to the principles of justice, equality, opportunity and optimism that Dr. King espoused and exemplified,"

George Bush declared in January 2003.

Then he went on to announce that his administration was joining the effort to destroy one of the lasting achievements of King's civil rights movement—affirmative action.

The Bush White House sided with white students suing the University of Michigan over an admissions procedure that they claimed was discriminatory because it gave preference to "unqualified" minority students. In a victory for supporters of civil rights, the U.S. Supreme Court decision on the case later that year stopped short of dismantling affirmative action. But the ruling continued the process of undermining the effort—once supported by the vast majority of Americans—to challenge centuries of racism and discrimination built into workplaces, schools, and other social institutions.

The backlash against affirmative action is a central point on the agenda of the right wing that all along was pulling the strings in the Bush administration. Bush campaigned as a "compassionate conservative." Yet his administration signed up with the organized racists behind the assault on affirmative action. It joined the bigots who went on the warpath over court rulings in 2003 that overturned anti-sodomy laws and gave gays and lesbians the right to marry in Massachusetts. And the White House put its full weight behind the anti-abortion fanatics determined to take away—restriction by restriction, medical procedure by medical procedure—a woman's right to choose abortion.

The common aim behind these attacks is to take away the political gains won by the social movements of the 1960s and 1970s. The conservatives' claim is that discrimination is a thing of the past—so measures to fight discrimination, such as affirmative action, are today giving certain minorities special privileges.

It's hard to see how anyone could really believe this. The Supreme Court decision that so incensed the antigay bigots in 2003, for example, overturned laws in thirteen states that made gay sex a criminal activity. Dollar for dollar, women still earn only 73 percent of what men do—and when measured by annual earnings (including those of part-time workers), women get just 59 cents for every dollar earned by men.

And anyone who thinks that racism is a relic of the past needs to take a look at what is laughably called the criminal "justice" system in the United States.

The U.S. passed a terrible new milestone at the end of 2002. It locked up its two millionth inmate in a jail or prison. More Americans are behind bars today than live in the cities of San Francisco, Boston, and Denver combined. The United States imprisons a higher proportion of its population than any country in history, according to the November Coalition.

To judge from such statistics, you'd assume that crime was running wild in the United States. Not true. Crime rates in virtually every category—including violent crime—decreased over the decade that followed the early 1990s. There's only one explanation for the skyrocketing prison population—the politicians' "tough on crime" hysteria. From the White House on down, politicians have competed to propose legislation that will crack down harder on criminals—no matter how insignificant the crime.

The main victims of the law-and-order brigade are by far racial minorities. One in every eight Black men between the ages of 20 and 34 is currently behind bars—an incredible seven times the rate for white men of the same age. Racism is especially obvious in the "war on drugs" that has filled prisons with nonviolent offenders. According to the Sentencing Project, African Americans are 13 percent of drug users in the United States, but they account for 35 percent of arrests for drug possession, 55 percent of convictions for possession, and 74 percent of those sentenced to prison for possession.

In Washington, D.C., young men from poor African American neighborhoods have a better than fifty-fifty chance of being under the supervision of the criminal justice system—either behind bars, on parole, or on probation. Imagine the turmoil if the statistics were even remotely similar in one of the better off, predominantly white areas of D.C. or its suburbs.

For most of the people warehoused in U.S. prisons, their real crime is having the wrong skin color—or simply being poor. This reality is plainest in the most barbaric face of the justice system—the death penalty. African Americans account for nearly 40 percent of prisoners on death row, three times their percentage in the overall U.S. population. More than 90 percent of defendants charged with capital crimes are too poor to afford an experienced lawyer to represent them.

Opinion polls show that personal attitudes about race have become less prejudiced in recent decades. But institutional racism still runs very deep. Aside from a small minority of middle-class African Americans who got the most benefits out of the reforms won by the 1960s civil rights movement, living conditions for the majority of Blacks aren't much better than they were thirty years ago. African Americans still regularly face terror at the hands of police forces steeped in racism. Unemployment for Blacks runs at twice the rate of the population as a whole, and African Americans are less likely to go to college.

We're told that America is the "land of opportunity"—that no matter where you start, if you work hard, you can make something of yourself. But America looks very different from the poverty-stricken, inner-city neighborhoods of this country. From there, it seems like no matter how hard you work, if you're Black and poor, you don't stand a chance.

Ultimately, this human waste is a price that the politicians are willing to see us pay. They may make pious statements about tolerance, but the system they preside over thrives on racism. For politicians, issues like crime—or the right-wing hysteria about gay marriage or illegal immigration—provide scapegoats that shift attention away from the real problems they do nothing about, like our crumbling schools or health care.

Scapegoating has a history as old as capitalism—for the simple reason that our rulers have to keep us divided in order to conquer. But more and more, people are seeing through the lies. The obvious fact is that we live in a class society—a world divided between the haves and have-nots.

CHAPTER TWO

A World of Wars

"Life is returning to normal for the Iraqi people," George W. Bush declared in a radio address in August 2003, five months after the United States invaded Iraq.

But not for Farah Fadhil. A few weeks after Bush's speech, the eighteen-year-old was killed—during a U.S. raid on an apartment complex in a town north of Baghdad. It was a slow and agonizing death. Farah's body was cut apart by shrapnel from a grenade tossed by U.S. soldiers. As she lay dying, the soldiers battered their way into her apartment, demanding to know—in English—where the Iraqi guerrilla fighters were hiding. But there was only Farah, bleeding to death on the floor in front of her mother and brother.

Why? Farah's family wanted to know. Did the U.S. learn that the complex had become, unbeknownst to them, a headquarters for the so-called "Saddam loyalists" resisting Washington's rule? "All we want are answers," says Qassam Hassan, a neighbor whose brother was killed in the same raid.

But answers there will never be. This story only came to light after a British journalist from the *Observer* newspaper learned about it from survivors. The Pentagon's press office in Iraq wouldn't even admit that the raid had taken place—much less offer an explanation for why Farah Fadhil had to die.

Farah is one among tens of thousands of Iraqis killed during the invasion and occupation of Iraq—though the Pentagon has acknowledged only a fraction of them. And she is but one among more than one million Iraqi victims of a U.S. war that has lasted not months, but years.

Life is not *returning* to "normal" for Iraqis. Life *remains* normal—because it has become "normal" for the Iraqi people to suffer death and devastation at the hands of the U.S. government.

In 1991, George Bush Sr. launched the first Gulf War over Saddam Hussein's invasion of Kuwait. For more than six weeks, U.S. and allied warplanes carried out the most intense aerial bombardment in the history of war. The slaughter ended with a brutal ground offensive against all-but-defenseless Iraqi conscript soldiers—and the "highway of death," when U.S. warplanes attacked anything that moved along the main road from Kuwait into Iraq, turning it into a mass graveyard of charred bodies and shattered vehicles.

In the years after, the United States continued to bomb Iraq at regular intervals, under Bush Sr., and then under Bill Clinton. But by far the majority of casualties died lingering and terrible deaths as a result of U.S.-backed economic sanctions imposed by the United Nations. The most basic goods—medicines, textbooks, fertilizers, chemicals for sanitizing water—were barred from the country. Human rights activists described epidemics of diseases caused by parasites that should have been easily treatable, except that hospitals in Iraq were chronically short of basic medicines and equipment. From one of the most economically advanced societies in the Middle East, Iraq was reduced to the level of poverty of the poorest countries in the world.

But that wasn't enough for George Bush Jr. He was planning a new war on Iraq from the moment he stole his way into the White House in 2001. Regime change in Iraq was "topic A" ten days after Bush's inauguration, according to former Treasury Secretary Paul O'Neill. "It was all about finding a way to do it," O'Neill said of early cabinet meetings.

In other words, the White House had its war plans ready and was waiting for the right moment. Then came September 11. While most people were still grappling with the enormity of the loss of life in the attacks on New York and Washington, D.C., the Bush administration saw its opportunity.

The war on "terrorism" became the all-purpose justification for expanding U.S. military power abroad and shredding civil liberties at home. First stop: Afghanistan, another country in the Bush administration's sights before September 11. After the Pentagon unleashed the world's deadliest arsenal against this poverty-stricken country devastated by two decades of warfare, Iraq was next.

Still cynically exploiting the tragedy of the 9/11 attacks, administration "hawks" openly admitted that a war in Iraq was just a first step in remaking the map of the Middle East. Washington's military machine won a quick victory after invading in March 2003. But the occupation that followed has been a different matter. Food remained scarce, with the whole of the population dependent on a ration system. Months after the invasion, Iraq's electricity and sewage systems remained in a shambles. Then there were the daily humiliations of life under U.S. occupation—pre-dawn raids, searches at gunpoint, military checkpoints, the chaos of violence and lawlessness.

It is difficult to describe what has taken place in Iraq for more than a decade—as a direct and conscious result of U.S. government policy under three presidents—as anything other than genocide.

And what is the justification? Saddam Hussein's weapons of mass destruction? They were cooked up by U.S. and British officials who knew they didn't exist, but needed an excuse for war. Iraq's connections to Osama bin Laden and "international terrorism"? Another lie. The liberation of Iraqis from the tyrant Saddam Hussein? This is the same dictator who was helped into power by the CIA. U.S. officials had no problems with Saddam when they handed over lists of Iraqi socialists to be hunted down and massacred by his Ba'ath Party. Washington backed Iraq during its war against Iran in 1980, and it looked the other way when he used chemical weapons against the Kurdish minority in Iraq.

U.S. policy changed only after Saddam invaded Kuwait in 1990—threatening the flow of Middle East oil. "If Kuwait grew carrots, we wouldn't give a damn," one former White House official admitted in the run-up to the first Gulf War.

Iraqis recognize that the United States is after oil and empire. So do growing numbers of U.S. soldiers, who were promised that they would be welcomed as liberators but instead have been cannon fodder for Washington's war makers. As Tim Predmore—at the time a soldier on active duty with the 101st Airborne and stationed in Iraq—wrote in an article for his hometown newspaper:

> This looks like a modern-day crusade not to free an oppressed people or to rid the world of a demonic dictator relentless in his pursuit of conquest and domination, but a crusade to control another nation's natural resource. At least for us here, oil seems to be the reason for our presence...I can no longer justify my service for what I believe to be half-truths and bold lies. My time is done, as well as that of many others with whom I serve. We have all faced death here without reason or justification.

The motives of the U.S. government in military conflicts are that plain—and have been since the United States emerged as a world power a century ago with its victory over Spain in the Spanish-American War. Even then, war supporters in Washington justified the fighting with rhetoric about liberating the subjects of Spain's colonial domination in the Caribbean and the Pacific. But the real aim of the U.S. was to be the new colonial boss—which is what it became in the former Spanish possessions of Cuba, Puerto Rico, the Philippines, and Guam.

The United States was late among the world's main powers in starting an empire, but it made up for that in violence. It started out in its own "backyard"—Latin America. Over the last century, U.S. troops have invaded Cuba five times, Honduras four times, Panama four times, the Dominican Republic twice, Haiti twice, Nicaragua twice, and Grenada once.

Eventually, American troops spread out around the world—conquering less powerful nations, but also fighting with other powerful countries over which would control what parts of the globe. The conflicts were both economic and military, but these empire-building—or imperialist—adventures never had anything to do with democracy and freedom.

Countries like the United States don't go to war to stop tyrants or for any of the other "humanitarian" reasons the politicians like to talk about. They go to war to preserve and expand their economic and political power.

General Smedley Butler's beat was Latin America. As a Marine Corps officer in the opening decades of the twentieth century, he headed a number of U.S. military interventions. Butler was under no illusion about what he was doing:

> I spent most of my time being a high-class muscle man for Big Business, for Wall Street and for the bankers. In short, I was a racketeer for capitalism.... Thus, I helped make Mexico and especially Tampico safe for American oil interests in 1914. I helped make Haiti and Cuba a decent place for the National City Bank to collect revenues in.... I helped purify Nicaragua for the international banking house of Brown Brothers in 1909–1912. I brought light to the Dominican Republic for American sugar interests in 1916. I helped make Honduras "right" for American fruit companies in 1903.

U.S. imperialism is no more kindly or charitable today. Socialists are accused of being "knee-jerk" opponents of U.S. imperialist adventures. And we are—because we believe that the U.S. government will never act except in the interests of injustice, tyranny, and greed. We believe that it's up to the people of Afghanistan, the Middle East, and elsewhere to settle accounts with local rulers and determine their own fates—free from the meddling of the "great powers."

With the invasion of Iraq and the war on Afghanistan, the Bush administration cranked up the U.S. war machine to a fever pitch. The so-called Bush Doctrine put forward by the White House is a vision of more extensive U.S. military involvement around the globe—"preemptive" wars waged to prevent the emergence of any rival to U.S. power, even in the distant future.

But it would be wrong to believe that the U.S. government before Bush Jr. was fundamentally more "peaceful"—or less committed to using military force to maintain U.S. power. For the last fifty years, not one day has passed in which the U.S. government has not had military forces committed around the world in one conflict or another. The difference between presidents—Republican and Democrat alike—has been a matter of tactics, and sometimes not even that.

We live in a world of wars. The Israeli state has carried out a relentless reign of terror against Palestinians, in the hopes of crushing all resistance to its occupation. In Latin America, the Colombian government has escalated its 40-year-old dirty war against left-wing rebels. In Asia, India and Pakistan—countries that recently tested nuclear weapons for the first time—have gone to the brink of all-out war over Kashmir, a small mountainous region claimed by both. Central Africa is the site of a horrific war that involves some of the world's poorest countries—Congo, Rwanda, Uganda, Zambia, Angola, and Zimbabwe.

The truth is that the U.S. government has had a hand—directly or indirectly, openly or covertly—in stoking these and many other conflicts around the world, sometimes supplying advice, sometimes guns, sometimes soldiers.

When weaker countries step out of line—by threatening a vital economic interest like Middle East oil, or by threatening the political balance of power in an important region, such as the Balkans in southeastern Europe—the U.S. and the world's other major powers will try to impose their domination. But the twentieth century has also seen two horrific world wars—not to mention dozens of smaller conflicts—that were battles *between* the major powers. At their root, these wars were also about economic power—about which imperialist country would dominate which areas of the globe.

Wars are a constant feature in the history of capitalism. They are the product of the ruthless competition for profit at the heart of the free-market system—of economic competition between bosses growing into political and military competition between countries.

That's why wars are inevitable under capitalism. Inevitable, that is, unless ordinary people fight back against the violence—and against a system that breeds war.

McDonald's and McDonnell Douglas

Guns and bombs are only one part of what socialists call "imperialism." The other side of the U.S. government's military reach into every corner of the globe is its domination—along with a handful of other powerful governments—of the world economic system. The two things go together—as *New York Times* columnist Thomas Friedman observed in 1998: "The hidden hand of the market will never work without a hidden fist. McDonald's cannot flourish without McDonnell Douglas, the designer of the F-15, and the hidden fist that keeps the world safe for Silicon Valley's technology is called the U.S. Army, Air Force, Navy and Marine Corps."

The gap between the winners and losers in the international economic order is immense. According to the United Nations' *Human Development Report, 2003*, income per person in fifty-four countries—more than one-quarter of the total—is *lower* now than it had been a decade before. Among the three-quarters of the world's population living in developing countries, one-third don't have clean water, one-quarter lack adequate housing, and one-fifth have no modern health services of any kind.

Whole areas of the globe seem to have been left to die by the capitalist system. In the desperately poor countries of sub-Saharan Africa, for example, the average household consumes 20 percent less than it did two decades ago. The AIDS epidemic is claiming literally millions of lives, and one out of every five children dies before the age of five.

In some of these countries, society has simply unraveled. Take Zambia, a country the size of Texas in central southern Africa. A dramatic fall in the world price for copper tore the heart out of the country's economy during the 1990s, and the result—coming amid the rising toll of the AIDS epidemic—has been outright barbarism. As of 2003, life expectancy stood at thirty-five years—nearly half of what it had been two decades ago. The odds of someone born in Zambia surviving to age sixty-five are ten to one against.

These are the consequences of a free-market system that benefits copper-buying multinational corporations and Zambia's own corrupt rulers at the expense of everyone else. And as if it weren't sick enough that human lives are at stake every time the price of copper falls, the International Monetary Fund (IMF) and the World Bank have tried to finish off Zambia.

The IMF and the World Bank are international financial institutions set up by the United States. They control whether poor countries receive desperately needed economic aid and loans—therefore, they have a blackmailer's power to demand government policies that they consider "appropriate."

During the early 1990s, IMF and World Bank officials decided that the government-run sector of Zambia's economy was "bloated"—too much government spending, too many programs to help the poor, too much state intrusion into the free market. The solution? One of the IMF's notorious "structural adjustment programs." The Zambian government was ordered to slash government spending and sell off state-run companies and services—including the crucial copper industry—to private buyers.

It's hard to imagine policies that could have done *more* damage. Zambia sold off state-run companies at a record pace, but half the newly privatized firms are bankrupt. According to human rights expert Mark Lynas, more than 60,000 workers lost their jobs as a direct result of structural adjustment—plunging up to half a million Zambians into destitution.

Masauso Phiri, who lives in one of the shantytowns that ring the capital of Lusaka, wonders if there's any point to going on. He lost his job as a security guard in the wave of layoffs that followed implementation of the IMF's structural adjustment program. "I know it's meant to put the economy on the right track," Masauso told Lynas. "But to me, it seems to make us suffer. We can't eat policies. I don't have any hope. I don't have any money, so I can't think of any future. My future is doomed."

A couple decades ago, it might have seemed like the worst flash points of poverty were in remote regions untouched by the modern economy. That isn't the case today. It's not unusual, even in central Africa, to find modern factories built by Western corporations side by side with miserable shantytowns—because the jobs don't pay a living wage.

Thus, as of 2001, the U.S.-based multinational Nike had thirty-three factories producing shoes, apparel, and equipment in the Southeast Asian country of Indonesia, with a combined workforce of 115,000 people. Four years earlier, when the legal minimum wage in Indonesia leapt to $2.47 a day, Nike bosses started having second thoughts. "There's concern what that does to the market—whether or not Indonesia could be reaching a point where it's pricing itself out of the market," said company spokesperson Jim Small. Fortunately for Nike, Indonesia was plunged into a severe financial crisis that year, and the legal minimum fell back below $1 a day.

Today, Indonesian workers who produce shoes and clothing for the immensely profitable Nike are among the 2.8 billion people in the world who survive on less than $2 a day.

Across the globe, the free market has produced more misery and suffering, not less—and not only in countries like Indonesia that have long been associated with dire poverty, but in nations that were thought to be on the road to industrial development and prosperity.

Case in point: Argentina. Throughout the 1990s, Argentina was the IMF's star pupil, embracing faster and more fully than any other country the so-called Washington model of privatization, free trade and investment policies, and sharp curbs on government spending. The Argentine economy did boom during the first half of the decade, based on massive borrowing from international investors.

Then the bottom fell out. In 1997, a financial panic that began in East Asia sent shock waves around the world, and foreign bankers who had been fueling the boom in Argentina pulled their money out. From poster child for the free market, Argentina began to fall into a 1930s-style depression. To avoid total collapse, the government asked for huge bailout loans. The IMF agreed—but with the condition that the government impose even deeper cuts in wages and social programs, which only made things worse.

In a country that once boasted the highest standard of living in Latin America, official government statistics showed in 2002 that half of Argentina's thirty-seven million people were living below the poverty line of $3 a day. Some 13 percent of the population suffered from malnutrition, and one study found that an average of twenty-seven children under the age of five died every day from causes related to hunger. This in a country that is the world's third-largest exporter of beef and second-largest exporter of wheat.

Argentina today is a symbol of the disaster of the free market. But it is also a symbol of something else—the spirit of resistance.

In December 2001, millions of Argentinians decided that enough was enough—and took to the streets of every city and town to demand that the government go. The demonstrations culminated in a massive turnout of more than one million people in the capital of Buenos Aires, a city of 2.7 million. The despised President Fernando de la Rúa was forced to quit—along with three more presidents in a period of two weeks.

The "Argentinazo" of December 2001 is a high point in the growing rejection of the free market—and a radical questioning of the assumptions that lay behind it. In Latin America, mass protests and huge strikes against privatization, trade agreements, and state violence have been regular occurrences—not only in Argentina, but in Venezuela, Colombia, Bolivia, Perú, Paraguay, Uruguay, Ecuador, Brazil, and Mexico. Argentina's revolt is part of a rising tide of struggle—across Latin America and around the world. Millions of people—from the poorest countries to the most advanced industrial powerhouses—have come to recognize that the capitalist system is failing them.

CHAPTER THREE

The Madness of the Free Market

There have always been rich and poor, in the United States and around the world. But the size of the gap between them has grown into a massive canyon.

At the end of the 1990s, the richest 0.01 percent of U.S. households—just 13,000 families—had a combined annual income as big as the poorest 20 million households. The richest 1 percent of families "earned" about as much as the bottom 40 percent of the population. And when it comes to wealth—the things that people own—the richest 2 percent of the U.S. population have a combined net worth equal to the other 98 percent.

Just how vast is the difference between the superrich and the rest of us? Think of it this way: Imagine we had a full year's wages for the average U.S. manufacturing worker—$32,181 in 2002, according to the Labor Department—in stacks of $20 bills. If we laid all the bills end to end, they would stretch 823 feet. That's a little more than one-eighth of a mile—about half a lap around a football field.

Now take Microsoft founder Bill Gates. Poor fellow lost

more than half his fortune after the 1990s stock market bubble burst, but he was still worth $40.7 billion in 2003, according to *Forbes* magazine's survey of the richest Americans.

If we had Gates's diminished fortune in $20 bills, laid end to end, they would stretch for 197,205 *miles.* That's about 800,000 laps around a football field. Or eight laps around the full circumference of the earth.

As of 2003, Bill Gates' fortune would stretch almost the distance from the earth to the moon.

Gates may be ahead of the pack, but the rest of the astronomically rich are doing fine. According to *Forbes,* there were 467 billionaires around the world in 2003, with a combined worth of $1.4 trillion. That's well above the combined gross national product of all the countries of sub-Saharan Africa, according to the World Bank—and roughly equal to the total annual income of the poorest half of the world's population.

That's 467 people with as much money as three billion people.

What could this tiny elite have done to deserve so much more than anyone else? We're often told that they worked for their fortunes. And at first glance, this might seem to apply to Gates, who wasn't born into billions.

But how did he get so rich? Did he work two million times harder than anyone else? Is he two million times smarter or two million times more enterprising? No. Bill Gates is rich because his company gained control of computer software developed by other people and successfully marketed it as the boom in personal computers took off in the 1980s. In other words, he was lucky.

E. Pierce Marshall, on the other hand, was lucky in a different way. He was lucky enough to be born the second son of oil baron J. Howard Marshall. And he was even luckier when his father died, leaving him a billion-dollar fortune. Pierce never had to do a day of work in his life—aside from squabbling with his brother and assorted other freeloaders over the loot. Yet E. Pierce Marshall has more money than 150,000 minimum-wage workers combined will make in a year of full-time work.

The truth is that the rich do nothing special to deserve so much more money than anyone else. In fact, they typically do nothing much at all. They almost never have anything to do with actually making or distributing products that people buy. Bill Gates doesn't assemble or package or transport or sell Microsoft products. He doesn't even come up with the software. Gates is rich because he *owns.* He and his fellow Microsoft shareholders own the means of producing computer software—the factories and offices, the machines, the patents on different technologies.

This is true about capitalism generally. A small class of people who own the "means of production" hire much larger numbers of people to do the actual work of making or providing different goods or services. The wealth of the few wouldn't exist without the labor of the many. The oil that's the source of E. Pierce Marshall's fortune, for instance, would still be in the ground.

For their labor, workers get paid a wage—higher or lower depending on the demand for their skills, whether they're in a union, and so on. But workers are never paid as much as they produce—usually, they're paid far less. The employers get to keep what's left over after they've covered wages and other costs of production, such as raw materials and machinery. This amount of money that they skim off for themselves is profit.

This is supposed to be fair—that workers get a "fair day's wage for a fair day's work," and employers get a reasonable return on their investments. But there's nothing fair about it. The employers have all the advantages. They have numerous ways to keep wages down, but there's no limit on their profits. Capitalism is built around organized theft—the theft of the value of what workers produce by the people who employ them.

The term that socialists use to describe this is "exploitation." That word is usually associated with especially low wages and terrible conditions. But exploitation goes on all the time. Every minute of the working day, a small class of people who do no productive work gets richer because it controls the goods and services produced by people who do work.

So as individuals, Bill Gates and E. Pierce Marshall may be lucky. But the social class that they belong to—the ruling capitalist class—doesn't rely on luck. It relies on a system that is organized to steal the wealth created by the vast majority—the working class.

Poverty in a world of plenty

Inequality isn't new. There have been rich and poor for thousands of years. What's different about the world today—as compared to, for example, the world that our ancestors lived in two hundred years ago—is that the resources exist to end poverty immediately.

Yet terrible poverty still exists alongside incredible wealth. The reason is that capitalism is designed to protect the rich and increase their wealth, no matter what the human cost.

Take the example of food production. According to the UN *Human Development Report, 2002,* more than six million children under the age of five die each year of malnutrition. The number six million has a terrible significance in the modern world—that is the number of Jews murdered by Germany's Nazis in the Holocaust during the Second World War. Incredibly, a holocaust of the world's children takes place every year—because of hunger.

How could this be? What could be the cause of such horror? Has there been some worldwide war of devastation or an international natural disaster that makes it impossible to produce enough food to go around?

In fact, the opposite is true. Even conservative estimates calculate that enough food is produced around the globe for everyone in the world to get 2,800 calories a day, well above the minimum standard set by the UN Food and Agriculture Organization. And this is food that already exists. According to one study, if the useable land of the world were cultivated effectively, the earth could feed more than forty billion people—six times more than the current world population and far more than are ever likely to inhabit the planet, according to scientific estimates.

The food exists to feed everyone. So there must be a problem in getting it to the desperately poor people around the world who need it. Again, no. Such a rescue effort wouldn't be beyond the capabilities of the world's most powerful countries. During the invasion of Iraq in 2003, for example, the

U.S. government spent about $1 billion a day, pouring troops, equipment, supplies, and weapons into the region. If the United States could mobilize this kind of operation to conquer an already devastated country, surely it could carry out an effort to save the lives of six million children.

But it doesn't. The sick reality is that nearly one billion people—one out of every eight people on the planet—are malnourished, not because there isn't enough food to feed them, but because they are too poor to afford it. "People are not hungry these days because food supplies are not available," the *Financial Times* newspaper admitted. "They are hungry because they are poor."

Instead of being organized to feed the hungry, the system of capitalism is organized around *not* feeding everyone. The owners and executives who control food production have an interest in keeping up prices—and therefore profits. So big agribusiness has conspired with governments around the advanced world to rig the system in its favor.

In 2003, the U.S. government spent nearly $20 billion on agricultural subsidies. Most of the money was used to prop up the price of grains and other crops by buying up "surplus" food. For example, U.S. farmers produce twice as much wheat as the U.S. market needs. This oversupply should cause the price for bread and other products to fall. But the government buys the excess to keep prices up.

The politicians claim that agricultural subsidies support "family farms" in the United States. That's a myth. According to the Environmental Working Group, 71 percent of farm subsidies since 1995 have gone to the top 10 percent of U.S. producers—the biggest agricultural operations, backed, if not owned outright, by multinational corporations.

Much of the food that the U.S. government buys is distributed around the world—in the form of food aid. But like everything else it does, Washington's motives are less than pure. Food aid is used as a weapon to promote U.S. interests—both politically, by providing the aid where it will help the geopolitical schemes of the U.S. government, and economically, where it will help pump up the profits of American corporations.

U.S. laws require that government food aid be distributed in the form of U.S.-grown products—even when those products exist in abundance in the country receiving the aid. Thus, in the early years of the decade, the United States sent more than one million metric tons of grain to the famine-plagued country of Ethiopia—even though Ethiopian farmers estimated that they had at least one hundred thousand metric tons of locally grown corn, wheat, sorghum, and beans rotting in warehouses because neither the government nor Ethiopians had the money to buy it.

Rather than feeding the hungry and helping countries struck by famine to develop agricultural production on their own, food aid from the U.S. government is mainly organized to help U.S. food bosses get rid of "surplus" food that might push down prices and profits. The effect is to keep food prices high at home and undercut competitors abroad, especially in developing countries—while the world's poor go hungry.

The German poet Bertolt Brecht might have had this sick system in mind when he wrote, "Famines do not simply occur—they are organized by the grain trade."

In the same way, you can say that poverty and inequality don't simply occur. They are organized by a tiny class of rulers at the top of society that benefits from the whole setup—increasing its wealth and power at the expense of the rest of us.

A system gone mad

For defenders of the free-market system, there's a simple response to Brecht's point: Dismiss it as a conspiracy theory. After all, talk about famines being "organized by the grain trade" sounds like something out of the *X-Files*—shadowy figures in back rooms hatching plots to dominate the world.

Actually, "conspiracies" do take place every day in Corporate America. Anyone who thinks otherwise needs to take a closer look at the collapse of the energy giant Enron at the end of 2001. Enron's bankruptcy revealed a mind-boggling range of scams—at a company that was the toast of Wall Street a few years before.

Some of the schemes were perfectly legal—for instance the creation of 3,500 subsidiary companies, including 900 in overseas tax havens like the Cayman Islands, as a way to avoid paying taxes. Others were outright frauds—like the practice, code-named "Death Star," of threatening to send electricity (which didn't actually exist) through overburdened transmission lines, forcing utility companies in California to pay off Enron to divert the fake electricity. As Enron executives wrote in a document that was released after the bankruptcy, "The net effect of [Death Star] transactions is that Enron gets paid for moving energy to relieve congestion without actually moving energy or relieving congestion."

Enron was far from the only respected corporate giant to cook the books or otherwise break the rules—as the string of corporate scandals that followed proves. Still, capitalism doesn't depend on conspiracies. Poverty and inequality are built into the structure of the system itself.

In theory, the capitalist free market is supposed to work according to the law of supply and demand. The basic idea is that capitalists control what gets produced and how, but they make their decisions according to what people buy. So consumers use their dollars as a sort of "vote"—and capitalists compete with each other to provide the products that consumers "vote" for.

But there's a problem at the heart of this theory: What if you don't have any money? Then you don't get a vote—and capitalists won't produce what you want.

In order for the free market to produce what's needed for everyone in society, there would have to be a roughly equal distribution of dollars to "vote" with. But in the real world, the rich have far more "votes" than anyone else. So the system is bound to put a priority on making products to meet their needs rather than the needs of society.

The result is a world where whole industries are devoted to products and services that are a total waste. Take advertising. Few people care all that much about the difference between Pepsi and Coke. But the owners and executives at the companies that produce the two soft drinks do—their profits depend on it. So they spend enormous sums trying to convince people to buy one over the other. Pepsi spent more than $2 million each for several 30-second-long commercials during the 2003 Super Bowl. Each ad cost more just to broadcast than a decently paid Teamster driver for Pepsi will earn in a lifetime of work.

And advertising is one of the more harmless forms of waste. Governments around the world spend nearly $1 trillion each year on their abilities to wage war. The U.S. government's military budget for 2003 was about $400 billion—more than the twenty next largest militaries *combined.*

The amounts of money spent on the Pentagon are staggering—but even more obscene is what this spending says about the priorities of the U.S. government. One B-2 stealth bomber costs the Pentagon $2.1 billion. That money could pay the salaries and benefits of 38,000 new elementary school teachers. The U.S. nuclear weapons program costs $16 billion a year, enough to provide health insurance for seven million U.S. children who are uninsured today.

So why does Washington keep squandering the money? One obvious answer is that filthy rich military contractors like Lockheed Martin and Raytheon depend on it—and they spend plenty of cash at election time to make sure their servants in Washington don't interfere with the Pentagon gravy train.

But there's a more important reason for the obscene amounts spent every year on the means to kill larger and larger numbers of people more effectively. Capitalism's blind drive for profit produces not only economic devastation, but military conflicts between different groups of national rulers. The drive to war is built into the system.

Looming over any talk of war in the twenty-first century is the threat of nuclear annihilation—a war fought with weapons that could destroy the basis of all life. But this nightmare isn't even limited to war. The everyday workings of the capitalist system wreak havoc on the environment.

Aside from a few "experts" who are paid off by the energy

industry to say otherwise, scientists are virtually unanimous in confirming that pollution from the burning of fossil fuels like coal and oil is leading to a small but significant increase in global temperatures. "Global warming" of even a few degrees will upset a delicate natural balance and have catastrophic consequences—widespread flooding, the spread of tropical diseases, terrible draughts, more severe weather conditions. Yet under the Texas oil boys who run the Bush administration, the U.S. government doesn't even acknowledge that climate change is taking place.

Any rational society would have long ago taken steps to stop this "greenhouse" effect. But even the international treaties designed to reduce emissions of greenhouse gases—the ones that the Bush administration has blocked—are insufficient for dealing with the problem. The sick truth is that it's profitable to pollute, even if that means devastation of the environment on a vast and irreversible scale.

This is the madness of the free market. Capitalism does one thing very well—it protects and increases the wealth of the people at the top of society. Meeting the needs of everyone else is secondary, which is why so many people's needs go unmet. From every other point of view—producing enough to go around, protecting the environment, building a society of equality and freedom—the capitalist system is entirely irrational.

From good times to hard times

Nothing exposes the madness of capitalism more clearly—and with more terrible consequences for huge numbers of people—than the regular economic recessions and depressions that plague the free-market system.

At the end of the 1990s, the politicians were celebrating what they called the U.S. "miracle" economy—the longest uninterrupted economic expansion on record. "They're shopping till they drop at the mall or on the Internet, happy as clams," *Business Week* magazine crowed at the beginning of 1999. The more enthusiastic pundits predicted that recessions were a thing of the past.

Within a few years, these "experts" were singing a different tune. The economic slump that officially began and ended in 2001 proved to be one of the most stubborn in history—with unemployment and declining wages and benefits continuing well into what was supposed to be a new upturn.

What happened? The commentators who were so smug and confident looked for scapegoats—maybe the corporate scandals, or the emergence of China as a growing exporter of cheap manufactured goods. But mostly, they were baffled.

This isn't unusual. Political and business leaders who take credit for the economic good times are quick to throw up their hands in a crisis. We're encouraged to think that economic slumps are just part of the way of things. In his novel about the auto industry, *The Fliver King,* writer Upton Sinclair described "people losing their jobs, and not being able to find others; it was something known as hard times; a natural phenomenon like winter itself, mysterious, universal, cruel."

But there's nothing "natural" or "mysterious" about capitalism's economic crises. They are the direct result of the drive for more profits—and what Karl Marx and Frederick Engels called a "crisis of overproduction." Marx and Engels believed that the headlong expansion of capitalism during economic good times laid the basis for slumps to come—because capitalists eventually produce more products than they can sell at an acceptable rate of profit. When profits begin to fall, the bosses rush to cut costs—and that means cutting back on investments, laying off workers and closing factories.

As Marx and Engels wrote in the *Communist Manifesto*:

> In these crises, there breaks out an epidemic that, in all earlier epochs, would have seemed an absurdity—the epidemic of overproduction. Society suddenly finds itself put back into a state of momentary barbarism; it appears as if a famine, a universal war of devastation had cut off the supply of every means of subsistence; industry and commerce seem to be destroyed. And why? Because there is too much civilization, too much means of subsistence, too much industry, too much commerce.

The *Communist Manifesto,* written more than 150 years ago, describes the U.S. economy today. During the 1990s, U.S. corporations dueled with one another in an unprecedented investment binge—in the hopes of capturing a bigger piece of a pie that seemed like it would never stop growing. The economy did grow, and Corporate America rang up megaprofits.

But the expansion created too much capacity—that is, it gave capitalists the capability to produce more products than they could sell at a price that would bring them an acceptable rate of profit. The problem is most obvious in telecommunications, where corporations made huge investments during the 1990s in fiber-optic cable and other equipment that was supposed to be the backbone of the "Internet revolution." But now that the Internet bubble has burst, only 5 or 10 percent of this capacity is being used, and the telecom giants are drowning in debt and slashing jobs.

Other industries are in the same bind. In the deserts of California and Arizona, more than 800 commercial airplanes sit in long rows, unused by U.S. airline companies that have laid off 120,000 workers. The auto industry worldwide has the capacity to manufacture eighty million vehicles a year, according to an analyst at Ford Motor Company, but global demand for new cars and trucks is only sixty million a year.

What is the response of auto companies? For one thing, they try to get rid of "excess capacity"—by laying off workers and closing down factories. They also face pressure to cut prices in the hopes of winning new customers at the expense of their competitors. The same factors are at work when overcapacity spreads. Layoffs and shutdowns at an auto company put pressure on the company's suppliers, which then cancel orders from their suppliers—and so on down the chain of the whole economy.

The result? "U.S. factory usage is at its lowest in more than twenty years; hundreds of jetliners are mothballed and the rest fly more than a quarter empty; rising apartment vacancies are forcing landlords to cut rents; and unemployment is at an eight-year high," the *Wall Street Journal* reported in the spring of 2003. "In short, too much supply is chasing too little demand."

Of course, there's a crying need for all the goods that are supposedly in "oversupply." If people are homeless on the streets of New York City, then there can't be "too much supply" of apartments and "too little demand" to fill vacancies. But because the capitalist economic system is organized around profits, the priorities of the system are topsy-turvy. From the standpoint of Corporate America, it is possible for there to be "too much supply," even when people go without—because there is "too much supply" to sell their products for a decent profit.

Food rots while people around the world go hungry. Shut-down steel mills rust as millions remain homeless. Computer factories close while schools—even in rich countries like the United States—lack the technology needed to teach students effectively. This is the reality of a system organized around making profits for the privileged few—no matter what the cost in terms of human misery.

CHAPTER FOUR

The Socialist Answer

Socialism is based on the idea that we should use the vast resources of society to meet people's needs.

It seems so obvious—if people are hungry, they should be fed; if people are homeless, we should build homes for them; if people are sick, all the advances in medical technology should be available to them. But capitalism produces the opposite.

To begin with, a socialist society would take the vast wealth of the rich and use it to meet the basic needs of all society. We'll take all the money wasted on weapons and war, and use it to end poverty and homelessness and all other forms of scarcity. We'll abolish advertising, and make sure that everyone can get a good education instead.

There's no blueprint for what a socialist society will look like—that will be determined by the generations to come who live in one. But it seems obvious that such a society would begin by guaranteeing that every family has enough to eat and a sturdy roof over its head. The education system would be made free—and reorganized so that every child's ability is encouraged. Health care would be made free and accessible, as would all utilities like gas and electricity. So would public transportation—and a far better funded and more efficient system it would be. This wouldn't be accomplished overnight. But these aims would become the top priorities of society.

A socialist society would not only take away the existing wealth of the ruling class, but also its economic control over the world. The means of production—the factories and offices and mines and so on—would be owned by all of society. Rather than leaving important economic decisions to the chaos of the free market and the blind competition of capitalists scrambling to make a profit, under socialism, the majority would plan what to do democratically.

The complaint from defenders of the capitalist system is that public ownership and planning would involve a bunch of bureaucrats ordering people around and telling them what they should want. But under capitalism, most people have few meaningful choices about the things that really matter in their lives—what they do at work and how they do it, what they can buy, how they spend the bulk of their time. These decisions are made in the corporate boardrooms, in the Oval Office, in the judges' chambers—without anyone being consulted.

The idea of socialist planning is based on the exact opposite—the widest possible discussion about what's needed in society and how to achieve it. Instead of leaving decisions about what gets produced and how to a handful of executives, all workers would have a voice in what they do at their workplaces. And larger bodies of democratically elected representatives would have a discussion about overall social priorities.

This isn't a guarantee that mistakes will never be made—that the planning process would never, for example, make more of one kind of product than people want, or not enough of another. But if a socialist society made such a mistake, we could *fix* it. We could give away the extra and shift resources to making something else. When capitalists make this kind of mistake—as they do constantly because of the blind competition of the market—factories are shut down, workers are thrown out on the street, food goes to waste to keep prices up. Socialism would put an end to these absurdities.

In order for planning to work, a socialist society must be democratic—much more democratic than the current system. Though we hear it all the time, it simply isn't true that democracy and capitalism go hand in hand. In fact, many of the models of the free market in the less-developed world are run by repressive dictatorships. Even in societies that brag about being democratic, democracy is limited to electing representatives every two or four years.

Socialism will be democratic in a more fundamental way. Unfortunately, the record of the former USSR, China, and other so-called "socialist" countries has left the impression that socialism is a top-down society run by party bosses. This has nothing to do with genuine socialism—or, for that matter, the whole experience of working-class struggle.

There have been many revolutionary upheavals during the last century—from the 1917 revolution in Russia, to Spain's revolution in the 1930s, to the Iranian revolution of 1979, to mention a few examples. And each one has created a similar system for the majority in society to make decisions about how to organize the struggle and what priorities to set. Each time, democracy revolved around a system of workers' councils.

In Russia, for example, workers' councils (known by the Russian word "soviets") developed spontaneously out of the 1905 revolution, and again in 1917. They first appeared as elected workplace committees, formed to organize over economic issues. But the need to respond to wider political questions led the councils to make links locally and then regionally.

It was natural for the soviets, created in the midst of struggles against the old order, to become the basis for workers to exercise their power in a new one. There was a direct connection between the councils' representation from workplaces and the need to decide how to use the wealth produced at those workplaces. And the level of grassroots participation was obvious from the ratio of soviet delegates to those they represented: one delegate for every five hundred workers.

As John Reed, an American socialist and author of *Ten Days That Shook the World*, an eyewitness account of Russia in 1917, described the spirit of the soviets: "No political body more sensitive and responsive to the popular will was ever invented. And this was necessary, for in time of revolution, the popular will changes with great rapidity."

Russia's soviets and all the examples of workers' councils in other countries over the years have shared common features: immediate recall, so workers can control those they elect; paying representatives no more than the people they represent and not allowing them to rise above anyone else's social level; elections taking place at mass meetings rather than in the isolation of the voting booth.

The exact shape of workers' councils in a future socialist society can't be predicted. What's important is the democratic principle that these councils have embodied in past struggles. The basic principle common to all revolutions is that representatives have to be held accountable to the people they represent. This can only be accomplished if discussion and argument thrive in every corner of society—and if representatives are responsible to the outcomes of these discussions. Such a system would be many times more democratic than what exists in today's world.

"Revolutionized from top to bottom"

The heart of socialism is making equality a reality. Marx and Engels summed up this aim with a simple slogan: "From each according to their ability, to each according to their need."

This concept infuriates the bosses and their ideologues. They can't grasp the idea of a society without power and privilege for a small group of people. They complain that under socialism, everyone would be paid the same. This is true. Roughly speaking, people would receive the same thing—there's simply no reason for it to work any other way. "Ah ha," comes the response. "You'd pay a brain surgeon the same as you pay a garbage collecor. Then no one would become a brain surgeon."

Think about what a statement like that says about the priorities of capitalist society. It says that the only reason people do the exacting work of trying to heal the sick is for money.

What a travesty! Socialism would be about giving people the opportunity to do what they really want to do—allowing them to become doctors or scientists or artists or anything else they desire. We would use our technological knowledge to eliminate thankless and unfulfilling jobs, like collecting garbage, as much as possible—and share out equally the tasks we couldn't. The goal would be to free all people to do the work they love—and to give them the leisure time to enjoy all the wonders of the world around them.

"It goes without saying that society cannot itself be free unless each individual is free," wrote Frederick Engels. "The old mode of production must therefore be revolutionized from top to bottom. Its place must be taken by an organization of production in which, on the one hand, no individual can put on to other persons his share of the productive labor...and in which, on the other hand, productive labor, instead of being a means to the subjection of men, will become a means to their emancipation, by giving each individual the opportunity to develop and exercise all his faculties."

Capitalism stifles people's creativity. Only a minority are asked to put their minds to thinking about society—and most of them do it for the purpose of making themselves richer, not for achieving any common good.

Imagine a society in which it mattered what ordinary people thought about what they were doing—where it mattered what an assembly-line worker thought about the pace of work, what a hospital worker thought about the availability of medical resources. That's a world in which people would become fully alive in a way they never will under capitalism.

CHAPTER FIVE

Can the System Be Fixed?

The basic idea of socialism—that the resources of society should be used to meet people's needs—seems so obvious. The real question is how to achieve it. How can society be transformed?

The realistic alternative, we're told, is to seek political change by working "through the system." After all, the U.S. government is supposed to represent the "will of the people." Therefore, those who want to make a difference should follow the democratic process and "work from within"—for example, by supporting political candidates they like, or even running for office themselves.

But the realistic alternative doesn't look very realistic in today's America.

First of all, after the 2000 presidential election, it's hard to say what the "will of the people" has to do with who has power in Washington. George W. Bush lost the popular vote in 2000 by half a million votes. But he won the White House anyway, thanks to a slim victory in the Electoral College, a relic of the eighteenth century designed to limit democracy and protect the interests of slaveowners—and ultimately, a 5–4 majority of the unelected justices of the U.S. Supreme Court, who decided that the state of Florida didn't need to count every ballot cast in the election.

The fraud in Florida followed a pathetic election campaign between Bush and Al Gore that offered little to choose from—two spin-doctored candidates, both financed by big business money, with more in common than not. When Ralph Nader's Green Party campaign posed a left-wing alternative, the two mainstream parties worked together to make sure Nader's voice wouldn't be heard in the presidential debates.

And they call this the "world's greatest democracy"?

Safely installed in power, Bush wasn't shy about serving the corporate interests that pumped $100 million into his presidential campaign—a figure that shattered all previous campaign finance records, though the Bush gang planned to double the take for 2004.

From the beginning, Bush's top domestic priority was tax cuts—not one, but two massive giveaways that together could cost over $2 trillion over ten years. Most of that money will end up in the pockets of the already rich. But the Bush administration has another aim, too. The tax breaks, along with increased military spending, ran up a massive budget deficit—and that will become the politicians' justification for slashing yet more funding for programs that benefit poor and working people.

Bush's priorities couldn't be more obvious—helping the rich and powerful get richer and more powerful still, at the expense of working people. But as brazen as it is, the Bush administration isn't unique—far from it. The truth is that all politicians, Republicans and Democrats alike, while they claim that they're answerable to "the people," are really answerable to the bosses who control U.S. society.

President Woodrow Wilson admitted as much at the beginning of the twentieth century:

> Suppose you go to Washington and try to get at your government. You will always find that while you are politely listened to, the men really consulted are the men who have the big stake—the big bankers, the big manufacturers and the big masters of commerce.... The masters of the government of the United States are the combined capitalists and manufacturers of the United States.

A century later, Wilson's words ring as true as ever. There's nothing subtle about the way Corporate America buys influence in Washington. Just look at the case of the bankrupt energy giant Enron.

Enron's previous success during the 1990s depended on having powerful friends in Washington. Friends like former Texas senator Phil Gramm, who received nearly $100,000 in direct donations from Enron and whose wife Wendy was hired onto the company's board of directors. Phil Gramm returned the favor when, as head of the Senate Banking Committee, he helped to push through legislation that exempted energy trading—Enron's core business—from government regulation. That allowed Enron and other giant power companies to inflate wholesale electricity prices. Consumers paid the price—especially in California, where the power bosses used a manufactured crisis to jack up utility bills and extort enormous sums from the state government.

Enron seemingly hit the jackpot when Bush was elected president. The company had been Bush's biggest financial backer by far since he first ran for Texas governor in the early 1990s. When Bush went to Washington, Enron CEO Ken Lay became the informal chief of energy policy for the U.S. government—at least until he and his bankrupt company became too much of an embarrassment to have hanging around the White House.

Like many corporate giants, Enron favored the Republicans for their legalized bribes. But Democrats like Bill Clinton made out as well—as long as they delivered on deregulation. In fact, the biggest players in Corporate America bet on both horses. Among the companies that contributed more than $1 million to both the Republicans and the Democrats during the 1990s were Archer Daniels Midland, ARCO Coal/Chemical, AT&T, Philip Morris, and RJR Nabisco.

It's obvious why money plays such an important role. Washington politics is about money. During the 2000 elections, for example, it cost on average $7.5 million to run a winning campaign for the U.S. Senate. The price tag on a seat in the House of Representatives was about $850,000. Obviously, that kind of money doesn't come from your average working person. According to Federal Election Commission statistics, business contributed more than 75 percent of the total donations to candidates and political parties during the 2000 election cycle. Unions, which are regularly denounced by Republicans for trying to control Washington, accounted for just over 5 percent.

Some of the same politicians who pocket big bucks from Corporate America complain about the influence of money on elections. But that's what makes the U.S. political system tick. "It's called buying access," said Matt Keller, of the campaign finance reform group Common Cause. "It doesn't matter if they're giving money to Trent Lott or Fred Flintstone. They're not giving for ideological reasons. They are giving for access reasons."

Corporate America certainly does expect access—and gets it. When the 2002 congressional elections gave the Republicans control over both houses of Congress, for example, business lobbyists rejoiced. The headlines from an election analysis sent out to investors by the brokerage firm Charles Schwab told the story: "More good news for the defense sector;" "For asbestos, the outlook is a little brighter;" "A plus for the tobacco industry;" "Broadcasters should benefit."

The message couldn't be clearer: Big business calls the shots in Washington.

Of course, winning an election also means getting ordinary people to vote for you, and no one would do that if the politicians were honest about their real work. All candidates—even the most dyed-in-the-wool Republican toadies for big business—talk about "serving the people" and giving ordinary Americans a better deal.

But this is a fraud—a fraud that reflects the basic nature of government under capitalism. The politicians are the public face of a system that's set up to serve the rich. Their job is to say one thing to the majority of people to win their votes—while doing another for their real masters.

Do the Democrats make a difference?

The U.S. political system is rigged in favor of the status quo. Elections today are more about perpetuating a common political power structure than choosing between real alternatives. That's why, in elections for the U.S. House in 1998 and 2000, 98 percent of incumbents won reelection—a higher rate than in the sham elections at the height of the Stalinist dictatorship in the ex-USSR.

Both Republicans and Democrats are responsible for this setup. But the two parties aren't exactly alike. On any given issue, most Republicans are likely to be more conservative than most Democrats. But the differences between the two parties are small when you compare them to the fundamental similarities that unite Republicans and Democrats.

Still, at election time, most people don't think about this. The differences are what seem to matter. The Democrats have the reputation of being the "party of the people"—the party that looks out for the interests of labor and minorities.

The truth is very different.

The Democrats' image dates back to the Great Depression of the 1930s and President Franklin Delano Roosevelt's New Deal reforms, which laid the basis for many of the programs we associate with the federal government today—like Social Security and unemployment insurance. These were important victories, and it's no wonder that workers look back on the politicians associated with them as friends of labor.

But that's not how Roosevelt thought of himself. "[T]hose who have property [fail] to realize that I am the best friend the profit system ever had," Roosevelt said. In fact, Roosevelt carried out the New Deal reforms as a conscious effort to head off a social revolt sparked by the Great Depression. In return, he got labor's votes—cementing the labor movement's misplaced loyalty to the Democrats that lasts to this day.

The Democrats played much the same role during the social upheavals of the 1960s. Presidents John F. Kennedy and Lyndon Johnson today have an entirely unearned reputation as antiracists because they eventually supported some civil rights reforms. But they had to be dragged into it. Kennedy did his best to ignore the growing civil rights movement in the U.S. South. And it was only after the Black struggle grew to explosive proportions that Johnson—a southern Democrat with a long record of opposing civil rights—pushed through the Civil Rights Act of 1964 and the Voting Rights Act of 1965, the two key pieces of 1960s civil rights legislation.

At the same time, the Democrats succeeded in co-opting some leaders of social movements, eventually putting them in the position of managing the system. Beginning in the late 1960s, for example, the number of Black Democrats holding political office grew to more than 10,000 elected officials. Most major U.S. cities have had an African American mayor for some period of time. But these politicians—elected with the hope that they would challenge racism—have carried out the same attacks as their predecessors.

In recent decades, the Democrats' record of actual accomplishments at the national level has grown even shorter—and Bill Clinton is the main case in point. After Bush's wars and right-wing fanaticism, many people now view the Clinton years with nostalgia. They're forgetting the real record—the long trail of broken promises that should serve as an object lesson in how Democrats will say one thing to win votes, then do another in office.

After all, when Clinton won the 1992 election, millions of people looked forward to his presidency with a sense of hope.

After twelve years of Republican presidents baldly attacking workers and the poor, Clinton was promising "change." He was going to fix the U.S. economy, then in the grips of a recession. He was going to reform the broken-down health care system. He was going to bring a sense of humanitarianism to American foreign policy.

But Clinton hadn't even entered the Oval Office before he began breaking promises—starting with pledges to end discrimination against gays and lesbians in the military and to grant asylum to Haitian refugees locked up at the U.S. naval base at Guantánamo Bay, Cuba. He didn't lift a finger as other parts of his agenda—like legislation to ban the use of scabs during strikes—went down to defeat in the Senate, controlled at the time by the Democrats.

Clinton took a full two years to screw up health care reform. With his wife Hillary Rodham Clinton leading the way, Clinton compromised away one provision after another in a failed attempt to appease the health care bosses. The final proposal was such a mess that congressional Republicans succeeded in portraying it as "big-government liberalism" run amok. Health care reform—the centerpiece of Clinton's 1992 campaign—never even came to a vote in Congress.

When the Democrats were routed by Republicans in the 1994 congressional elections—mainly because of disillusionment with his broken promises—Clinton was written off as a lame duck. But he managed a comeback—not by challenging Republican attacks, but by stealing the Republican program and offering a gentler version of it.

The legislation that Clinton signed into law in the years that followed was, in many cases, worse than anything that

Ronald Reagan or George Bush Sr. managed. Clinton's two "crime bills" massively expanded the federal death penalty system, set off a prison-building boom, and poured money into hiring more police. And in 1996—in the middle of his re-election campaign—Clinton signed the Republicans' version of welfare "reform."

The GOP was furious. "The good news is that we're going to have a Republican president in 1996," snarled one disgruntled Republican. "The bad news is that it will be Bill Clinton."

This is the real record that so many people who look back fondly on the Clinton years forget. Yet in spite of his broken promises, Bill Clinton had the uninterrupted support of organized labor and liberal organizations for as long as he was in the White House. In fact, at various points, these groups disarmed opposition to Clinton's "Republican Lite" policies.

In the case of welfare "reform," for example, liberal organizations that could have organized a response insisted that it was more important to stand behind Clinton for fear of getting something worse—a Republican victory in the 1996 election. "This is a bad bill, but a good strategy," said Representative Gary Ackerman (D-N.Y.), explaining why he was voting for the welfare bill that he opposed. "In order to continue economic and social progress, we must keep President Clinton in office.... Sometimes, in order to make progress and move ahead, you have to stand up and do the wrong thing."

This is a perfect example of the politics of "lesser evilism"—the idea that people who believe in ideals of justice and peace should hold their nose and vote for Democrats, who believe in neither, as the lesser evil, in order to avoid the greater evil of a Republican victory.

It's certainly understandable why people disgusted by Bush would want to stop the Republicans at any cost. Supporting the Democrats, not in the hope that they will accomplish anything, but that they will stop something worse from happening, seems sensible.

In reality, this is exactly the wrong way to stop the "worst" from happening—as all the people who voted for Bill Clinton because they hated the Republican's cruel, victim-blaming proposals to wreck welfare should remember now.

The distance between Democrats and Republicans is not nearly so large as the distance that the two parties *together* have shifted to the right over the course of the last twenty-five years. If Clinton's record looks rosier compared to Bush's, it shouldn't be forgotten that Clinton stands out as *more* conservative than presidents who came before him—Republicans included. So, for example, Republican President Richard Nixon launched more antidiscrimination and affirmative action programs than Bill Clinton. That's not because Nixon was more liberal—on the contrary, he was a miserable right-winger. But Nixon was under pressure to act from the mass social movements of the 1960s and early 1970s—something that Clinton never faced.

As the historian Howard Zinn put it in an interview with *Socialist Worker* newspaper right after George W. Bush took office, "There's hardly anything more important that people can learn than the fact that the really critical thing isn't who is sitting in the White House, but who is *sitting in*—in the streets, in the cafeterias, in the halls of government, in the factories. Who is protesting, who is occupying offices and demonstrating—those are the things that determine what happens."

The problem with voting for the lesser evil is that you usually get the lesser and the greater evil together. Democrats like Clinton won't make any concessions to our side if they know that we're in their back pocket. They will always shift to their right, appealing to so-called swing voters, if they think that they can take the support of those to their left for granted.

That's why we need a working-class alternative to the twin parties of capitalism.

The limits of reform

In 2000, Ralph Nader's presidential campaign gave people in the United States an opportunity to vote for a genuine left-wing alternative for the first time in half a century. Even though Democrats slandered Nader mercilessly for "stealing" votes from Al Gore, his campaign was a lightning rod for millions of people fed up with a political system that offers so little choice.

But while it's better to be able to vote for a candidate who stands for what we believe in rather than the interests of Corporate America, voting isn't the most important way to be politically active. Ultimately, socialism can't come through the ballot box.

We're encouraged to believe that the government is a neutral force in society—that it can stand above competing groups and make fair and even-handed laws that treat everyone equally. That's an illusion. Governments in capitalist societies aren't even-handed at all. They ultimately act in the interests of the ruling class. One reason is because the bosses dominate the system of legalized bribery that funds the mainstream political parties—so they have a lot bigger say in what our elected representatives decide to do.

But there's more to the question. Governments consist of more than elected representatives. There are the unelected bureaucracies that make crucial decisions affecting people's lives. There's the judicial side of the U.S. government—federal judges all the way up to the Supreme Court never face an election. And standing behind all this is what Frederick Engels called "bodies of armed men"—the police and the army. Formally, the Pentagon may be answerable to elected politicians. But in reality, it's a power unto itself.

Because of this, even politicians with every intention of "making a difference" find that rather than being able to pull the levers of power to change the system, the levers of power pull them. They end up managing the system they expected to change.

Suppose you were elected president and were determined to impose a tax on the rich to pay for a system of universal health care. Within minutes of taking office, you would get a visit from your treasury secretary, who at least you had appointed, and the chair of the government's central bank, the Federal Reserve, who you didn't have any say about. They would tell you that Wall Street wanted nothing to do with your plan unless you compromised. If you persisted, the bosses would take further action—sending their money out of the country so it couldn't be taxed and causing turbulence on the financial markets until you said "uncle."

The "realistic" response would be to make concessions—to try to find some arrangement that would be acceptable to all sides. But when this becomes the priority, politics turns into the art of compromise rather than a campaign to accomplish something. And that shapes the plans and outlook of the people trying to make change in a system rigged against them.

Beyond all these considerations, the fact is that many of the most important decisions about people's lives have nothing to do with elected officials. Politicians don't vote for layoffs at a big U.S. corporation. The only people who have a say in that decision are corporate executives—answerable, if at all, to the tiny handful of people rich enough to own a significant chunk of the company's stock.

Elected representatives are only one part of government under capitalism. And in a number of tragic examples in countries around the world, they've turned out to be the dispensable part—when sections of the ruling class have decided to ditch democracy and rule by force.

The most infamous case of this comes from Chile. The socialist Salvador Allende was elected president in 1970 on a fairly mild program of reform that included nationalizing parts of the economy. Many people took this as a sign that socialism could be elected into power. But for the next three years, Chile's bosses—and their international partners, especially in the United States—did everything they could to sabotage Allende. U.S. Secretary of State Henry Kissinger declared: "I don't see why we need to stand by and watch a country go communist because of the irresponsibility of its own people."

Allende did compromise. But that wasn't enough. When the time was ripe, Chile's generals made their move—launching a bloody coup that claimed the lives of tens of thousands of Chilean workers, along with Allende's.

Our rulers prefer to dominate a political system that provides the appearance of democracy but gives them most of the influence over what decisions get made and how. But if any force arises to threaten this rule, they have been willing to dispense with democracy—and rule by brute force.

That's why socialists believe that the system can't be reformed. Even if they weren't bought off, political leaders don't have the power to really transform society. Instead of trying to get well-intentioned politicians elected to make what changes they can, we need to overturn the whole system.

That is what a revolution is about. It is about taking away the power of the people at the top of society to make unaccountable decisions that affect our lives. It is about getting rid of a state machine organized to preserve the system as it exists today. And it is about organizing a completely different and more democratic system to make decisions about society.

This doesn't mean that socialists don't care about reforms. In fact, short of revolutionary upheavals, socialists spend most of their efforts mobilizing pressure to win changes in the existing system. Socialists have played a central role in all kinds of struggles aimed at winning seemingly small reforms in the here and now—civil rights for African Americans, the right of workers to organize unions, women's right to choose abortion. These reforms make workers' lives easier and increase their power. They make people more confident in the struggle to win further change. As the revolutionary Rosa Luxemburg wrote:

> Can we counterpose the social revolution, the transformation of the existing social order, our final goal, to social reforms? Certainly not. The daily struggle for reforms, for the amelio-

> ration of the condition of the workers within the framework of the existing social order, and for democratic institutions, offers to [socialists] the only means of engaging in the proletarian class war and working in the direction of the final goal—the conquest of political power and the suppression of wage labor. Between social reforms and revolution there exists...an indissoluble tie. The struggle for reforms is its means; the social revolution, its aim.

Socialists fight for reforms. But reforms by themselves aren't enough—because they can be taken back if the movement retreats. We need revolution because capitalist society can't be permanently changed in any other way.

CHAPTER SIX

"If There Is No Struggle, There Is No Progress"

When socialists talk about the need for a revolution to fundamentally transform society, we're often accused of being unrealistic and utopian. The argument starts in different ways—people are bought off by the system, they're made stupid by television and popular culture, the U.S. government itself is so powerful that it can't be challenged. But it always ends with the question: How can a revolution ever take place in the United States?

Actually, the question isn't *whether* a revolution can take place in the United States. The question is whether *another* revolution can take place.

The United States has already had two revolutions. The first, in 1776, overthrew colonial rule by Britain's monarchy. That struggle spread to every corner of society and produced a new nation, organized around a representative government and perhaps the widest system of democracy known to the world to that point. True, there were gaping holes—the terrible crime of slavery was left untouched. But the new United States was an advance over what had come before.

The U.S. experienced another social revolution ninety years later—the Civil War of 1861–65, which destroyed the Southern system of slavery. Today, credit for "freeing the slaves" usually goes to Abraham Lincoln and perhaps a few army generals. But the North would never have won the war against slavery without the active participation of masses of people. Black slaves themselves played a crucial role in the struggle, as did the agitators of the abolitionist movement in the North. Also central to the transformation were the soldiers of the Northern army—many of whom started without a clear idea of the war's aim, but were convinced over time of the need to abolish slavery.

These were not *socialist* revolutions. The War of 1776 and the Civil War were revolutions against colonial rule and against slavery, which left the economic setup of capitalism intact. Nevertheless, these struggles fundamentally transformed U.S. society—and disprove the picture of a country that has always been stable and united.

What's more, the years since have produced other uprisings that shook this country to its foundations—the struggle for the eight-hour day during the 1880s; the "great red year" of 1919, when one in five U.S. workers was on strike; the 1930s struggles to win mass unionization; and the 1960s, which opened with the civil rights movement in the South and closed with struggles that questioned almost everything about U.S. society, from the brutal war in Vietnam to the oppression of women and gays and lesbians.

This way of looking at the past is very different from what passes for history in school. To begin with, the way history is usually taught—remembering the names of famous people and the dates when they did something important—is upside down. The course of history depends, first and foremost, not on what a few "great men" did or thought, but on the actions of huge numbers of people, especially during the times when they organize themselves in rebellions and revolutions. It's not that figures like George Washington and Abraham Lincoln are unimportant. But what they did and what they're remembered for today was shaped by the actions of masses of people who aren't remembered at all.

Bertolt Brecht made this point in a poem called "Questions from a Worker Who Reads":

> Who built Thebes of the seven gates?
> In the books you will find the names of kings.
> Did the kings haul up the lumps of rock?
> And Babylon, many times demolished.
> Who raised it up so many times? In what houses
> Of gold-glittering Lima did the builders live?
> Where, the evening that the Wall of China was finished
> Did the masons go?...
>
> The young Alexander conquered India.
> Was he alone?
> Caesar beat the Gauls.
> Did he not have even a cook with him?
> Philip of Spain wept when his armada
> Went down. Was he the only one to weep?
> Frederick the Second won the Seven Years' War. Who
> Else won it?
>
> Every page a victory.
> Who cooked the feast for the victors?
> Every ten years a great man.
> Who paid the bill?

Something else flows from a socialist view of history. We're told that political and social change—if it happens at all—takes place at a safe, gradual pace. Let any group of people organize to show their opposition to an injustice, and they're certain to be told to be patient—to let the system work. But this goes against the whole history of the struggle for justice and equality. In the first half of the nineteenth century, virtually every U.S. politician, North and South, believed that the enslavement of Blacks would die out eventually if the Southern slave system were left alone. Yet the slaveholders' power only grew. It took a civil war to put an end to this horror.

The United States is supposed to be the most stable of countries. But revolutions and social upheavals are a constant theme. Most of the reforms that workers take for granted today are a product of those upheavals. Unemployment insurance, for example, was introduced as part of President Franklin Roosevelt's New Deal program of the 1930s. Roosevelt didn't come up with the idea. He was forced by the crisis of the Great Depression and by massive social pressure to adopt an idea put forward by workers.

Political leaders like Roosevelt always end up with credit in the history books for reforms they were forced to carry out. But this doesn't change the fact that they were *forced* to act.

Struggle is the key. The great abolitionist leader Frederick Douglass made this plain with these words:

> The whole history of the progress of human liberty shows that all concessions yet made to her august claims have been born of earnest struggle.... If there is no struggle, there is no progress. Those who profess to favor freedom and yet deprecate agitation are men who want crops without plowing up the ground, they want rain without thunder and lightning. They want the ocean without the awful roar of its mighty wa-

ters. The struggle may be a moral one, or it may be a physical one, and it may be both moral and physical, but it must be a struggle. Power concedes nothing without a demand. It never did, and it never will.

A power greater than their hoarded gold

For hundreds if not thousands of years, most societies around the world have been divided between exploiters and exploited—between a ruling class of people that runs society in its own interest and much larger exploited classes whose labor is the source of their rulers' wealth and power. Under each system, the biggest conflicts have been between these classes—over who rules, who gets ruled over, and how. As Karl Marx and Frederick Engels put it in the *Communist Manifesto*:

> The history of all hitherto existing society is the history of class struggles. Freeman and slave, patrician and plebeian, lord and serf, guildmaster and journeyman, in a word, oppressor and oppressed, stood in constant opposition to one another, carried on an uninterrupted, now hidden, now open fight...

The oppressed have always dreamed of a future world of equality and justice where their oppression would end. And they have fought for it—from the slave rebellion against the Roman Empire led by Spartacus to the peasant uprisings in Europe, among others.

So the ideals of socialism aren't new. But the possibility of achieving them is the product of only the last few centuries—in most parts of the world, of just the last one hundred years.

Why? Because socialism can't be organized on the basis

of scarcity. Unless there's enough to go around, there's certain to be a scramble over who gets what. That scramble is bound to produce a class society—a society in which one group of people organizes the system to make sure they get enough, even if others go without. Only under capitalism has human knowledge and technology been raised to the point that we could feed every person on the planet, clothe them, put a roof over their heads, and so on.

So under capitalism, there's no longer any natural reason for poverty to exist. But abolishing poverty means getting rid of a system that causes it—and that requires a social force capable of overthrowing it. Marx and Engels argued that in the process of its development, capitalism produced "its own gravediggers"—the working class, with the power to overthrow the system and establish a new society not divided between rulers and ruled.

Why did Marx and Engels talk about the working class? Not because workers suffer the most under capitalism or because they're morally superior. Socialists focus on the position that workers occupy in the capitalist economy. Their labor produces the profits that make the system tick.

Among activists today, few would dismiss the importance of unions and other workers' organizations being involved in struggles such as the global justice movement. But for many, labor seems like just another movement—one in a long list of "causes." This misses something important. The working class as a whole has a special power to paralyze the system that no other social group has—to bring the profit system to a halt by not working.

You can see this power in situations that fall well short of revolution. In 1996, for example, General Motors (GM) provoked a strike of 3,200 autoworkers at two Dayton, Ohio, factories that made brake parts for most GM vehicles. It was a huge blunder. Within a week, the walkout had crippled GM's production across North America. All but two of the company's assembly plants had to close down. In fifteen days, GM lost about $1 billion in profits. Management gave in.

Because of their economic role, struggles that involve workers exercising their power as workers can have a deeper impact. That was the case in apartheid South Africa, for example—where the rise of Black workers' struggles in the 1980s shook the system more dramatically than all the battles that had come before, ushering in the final days of the racist regime.

A *general* strike by workers throughout the economy can paralyze a whole country—and bring a government to its knees. That's what happened in Poland in 1980 with the revolt of the Solidarnosc trade union. The upheaval began with a strike by shipyard workers in Gdansk, but it soon spread to involve ten million workers across the country. Within weeks, democratically organized workers' committees sprang up to organize the strike and make decisions about how to provide essential services. The so-called "socialist" government—a dictatorial regime with a long record of repression—was powerless to restore order for more than a year.

Before the strike, Polish workers would never have guessed that they could rock a seemingly all-powerful police state. But they cut off the lifeblood of the system—the wealth that they created with their labor.

Of course, other groups in capitalist society can and do fight back. For example, during the 1960s, the biggest upheavals in the United States involved African Americans fighting for civil rights and against racism. These were magnificent struggles that won real and lasting changes. But by themselves, Blacks didn't have the power to transform the whole system. First, they were a minority of the population. And organized as a community, African Americans had the moral power to embarrass and persuade—but not the economic power to hit the bosses where it hurts.

Struggles organized on the basis of class have the potential of uniting the working majority throughout society. They hold out the promise of overcoming divisions among the have-nots so that they fight on a common basis—not only for the demands they have in common, but for the special demands of specific groups.

Workers only have power if they're united. "Labor in white skin cannot emancipate itself where it is branded in Black skin," Marx wrote about slavery in the United States. The point can be extended to every form of bigotry and discrimination. That's why it's crucial for socialists to champion all fights against oppression. These struggles are just in their own right. But they're also critical in building working-class unity.

"Solidarity forever" and "An injury to one is an injury to all" are old slogans of the labor movement. But they're more than good ideas. They are absolutely necessary for workers to win.

One of the most common criticisms of Marxism is that the working class has been shrinking in importance and numbers as capitalism has aged. What people who say this really mean is that in advanced countries, the blue-collar industrial working class has been decreasing as a proportion of the workforce as a whole. But internationally, the size of the industrial working class is bigger than ever—and even in advanced countries, it remains an important part of the economy.

More importantly, though, the idea that Marxists only care about blue-collar workers is a stereotype—one that goes along with a picture of the "proletariat" as all male, working only in factories, engaged in manual labor. From the beginning, Marx defined the working class not by the kind of work people did, but by their position in society—as "a class of laborers who live only so long as they find work, and who find work only so long as their labor increases capital," he wrote. In other words, the working class consists of people who have to sell their ability to work in order to survive. Obviously, this applies not only to blue-collar factory workers, but to people who work in offices or the service sector.

So when Marxists talk about the working class, we don't mean a minority of people who fit into the narrow blue-collar occupation category. We mean the vast majority of people in society—in a country like the United States, something like 75 percent of the population. And this applies around the world, even in poor countries that a couple of decades ago didn't seem to fit the picture at all.

Nearly every country in the world today has a big working class. And what's more, the struggles of recent decades have shown the emergence of the working class in the less-developed world as a social force. It's impossible, for example, to talk about the revolution that toppled the dictator Suharto in Indonesia in 1998 without recognizing the role of the new working-class movement.

When Marx and Engels were writing in the middle of the ninteenth century, the international working class was tiny—perhaps two or three million people, concentrated in Britain, a few countries in northwestern Europe, and along the northeastern coast of the United States. Today, there are more workers in South Korea than there were around the world in Marx and Engels' time.

Everywhere across the globe, people's lives are shaped by the fact that they have to work for a boss in order to survive. But the flip side of this reality is that workers have enormous power. The final words of the *Communist Manifesto* are more relevant today than ever before: "The proletarians have nothing to lose but their chains. They have a world to win."

Can workers change society?

If we were to judge only from what we see around us, it might be hard to have confidence that the majority of people can organize to win fundamental change. After all, most working people aren't revolutionaries. Actually, a significant number—at the least, a sizeable minority—vote for George Bush's Republicans during elections. And even for those who oppose the Republicans' pro-corporate agenda, they accept a number of ideas that justify the status quo most of the time—from the old cliché that you can't fight city hall to the belief that people at the top of society are somehow specially qualified to run it.

This is partly because we're continually exposed to different institutions that are in the business of reinforcing these prejudices. The mass media are one example. Watch the local television news, and you'll see sensationalized stories about crime and violence—while discussion about the issues that affect people's lives gets shortchanged. The poor are stereotyped and scapegoated, while the wealth and power of the rich are celebrated. Even shows meant as entertainment tend to reinforce the conventional wisdom.

Likewise, it's easy to see how the education system encourages conformity. Except for the minority of students being trained to rule society, the experience of school is usually alienating. Students are taught to compete against each other—and ultimately to accept the conditions they see around them.

With all the selfish and mean-spirited ideas actively promoted by these voices of authority, it's a wonder that any sense of solidarity survives under capitalism. But it plainly does. This is most obvious in the outpourings of charity in cases of social disasters, like famines or earthquakes—even when they take place halfway around the world.

The kindness and generosity of ordinary people can be extraordinary in these situations. But even on a day-to-day basis, society simply couldn't function without a basic sense of cooperation and sacrifice among ordinary people—within families, for example, or among coworkers.

The point is that capitalist society obscures this basic decency—because the system is organized around greed. Obviously, those in charge get ahead by being as greedy as possible. But working people are forced—whether they like it or not—to participate in a rat race that they have no control over. They're pitted against one another and required to compete just to keep their jobs or maintain their standards of living.

As a result, the idea of people uniting for social change can seem distant and unrealistic. For most people, the experience of their lives teaches them that they don't have any power over what happens in the world—and that they don't know enough to have an opinion about it anyway. Powerlessness produces what appears to be apathy among people—about their own future and the future of society.

This is why it isn't enough for socialists to talk about why socialism will make an excellent alternative to capitalism. It's also necessary to talk about the struggle to get there—because struggle transforms people and gives them confidence in their own power. As Karl Marx put it, "Revolution is necessary not only because the ruling class cannot be overthrown in any other way, but also because the class overthrowing it can only in a revolution succeed in ridding itself of all the muck of ages and become fit to found society anew."

The act of fighting back is the first step in challenging the prejudices learned from living in the dog-eat-dog world of capitalism. This can be seen in even a small strike. Strikes almost always start over a specific workplace issue—demands around wages and benefits, for example. But whatever the original grievance, striking workers who may have thought of themselves as law-abiding citizens are acting in a way that goes against what society teaches them.

Fighting back also requires unity. So striking workers are often forced to question the divisions built up in their ranks—between Black and white, between men and women, between native born and immigrant. As the strike goes on, feelings of solidarity and a sense of the wider issues at stake start to become as important as the original issues.

The changes that take place are profound. Take the "War Zone" labor struggles in Illinois in the mid-1990s. The center of the War Zone was in Decatur, a small industrial city where workers were on strike or locked out at three companies—the food processor A.E. Staley, the heavy equipment manufacturer Caterpillar, and tire-maker Bridgestone-Firestone.

Several months into the struggles, activists organized a multiracial march to celebrate Martin Luther King's birthday—in a town where the Ku Klux Klan had organized not many years before. The War Zone workers were drawing on King's statements about the fight for civil rights to explain what their own struggles were about—and to show that they had come to see that their fight for justice in the workplace was linked to other struggles in society.

In the course of any struggle, activists committed to the fight around a particular issue have to grapple with questions about their aims—what kind of change they want and how to achieve it. Their answers evolve with their experiences.

Think of the Black college students who joined the civil rights movement in the 1960s. In 1960, one member of the newly formed Student Nonviolent Coordinating Committee (SNCC) could tell a reporter that she was motivated by traditional American values. If only Blacks were given educational opportunities, she said, "maybe someday, a Negro will invent one of our [nuclear] missiles."

A few years later, many SNCC members considered themselves revolutionaries. They had been through the Freedom Rides to desegregate interstate bus lines, the murder of civil rights workers during the Freedom Summer voter registration project in 1964, and the Democratic

Party's betrayal of civil rights delegates at its 1964 national convention. These experiences convinced them that the struggle against racial injustice could only be won by linking it to the fight against other injustices—and for a different kind of society altogether.

This transformation was repeated throughout the 1960s and early 1970s. White college students who volunteered for Freedom Summer used the skills they learned from the civil rights movement to organize the struggle against the U.S. war in Vietnam. Veterans of the antiwar movement in turn launched the struggle for women's rights, including the right to choose abortion. The modern gay and lesbian movement was born in 1969 with the formation of the Gay Liberation Front—an organization named after the liberation army in Vietnam.

Though the media love to dismiss them today, the struggles of the 1960s are proof that ideas can change with enormous speed. In periods of social upheaval, millions upon millions of people who focused their energy on all sorts of other things suddenly turn their attention to the question of transforming society.

The biggest struggles of all—revolutions that overturn the existing social order—produce the most extraordinary changes in people. What's most striking about the history of revolutions is the way that ordinary people—trained all their lives to be docile and obedient—suddenly find their voice.

The caricature of revolution passed off by many historians is of a small group of armed fanatics seizing control of the government and running it to enrich themselves. But this has nothing to do with genuine socialism. A socialist revolution can't be carried out by a minority—even a minority that genuinely wants to improve the lives of the majority. That's because the heart of socialism is mass participation. As the Russian revolutionary Leon Trotsky put it:

> The most indubitable feature of a revolution is the direct interference of the masses in historic events. In ordinary times, the state—be it monarchical or democratic—elevates itself above the nation, and history is made by specialists in that line of business—kings, ministers, bureaucrats, parliamentarians, journalists. But at those crucial moments when the old order becomes no longer endurable to the masses, they break over the barriers excluding them from the political arena, sweep aside their traditional representatives, and create by their own interference the initial groundwork for a new regime.... The history of a revolution is for us, first of all, a history of the forcible entrance of the masses into the realm of rulership over their own destiny.

The right-wing writers who pass judgment on revolutions also tend to focus on the endpoint—the armed insurrection to topple a government and seize political control. But this is only the final act of a revolution. It's the climax of a much longer period of struggle in which the rulers of society face a growing crisis—at the same time as workers become more confident of their own power.

At the beginning of the process, the goals for change can be modest—a few reforms in the way the system operates. But the struggle to change this or that aspect of society raises deeper questions. People begin to see the connections between the struggles that they're involved in and other issues—and the nature of the system itself. Each of these struggles gives workers a further sense of their ability to run society for themselves. The act of taking over political power is the final step of a revolution that has already been felt in every workplace, in every neighborhood, and in every corner of society.

Ten days that shook the world

The Russian Revolution of 1917 is the only socialist revolution so far to succeed and survive for any length of time. Though the experience of workers' power was brief—a matter of less than ten years before the revolution was defeated—it offers a glimpse of what socialism will look like.

Because of this, the Russian Revolution has been the subject of countless lies and slanders. Chief among them is the idea that the 1917 revolution was a coup, organized by the master manipulators Lenin and Trotsky. Nothing could be further from the truth. The seeds of the revolution lay in the mass hatred of Russia's tsar—and the misery of poverty and war that the tsar presided over. The Russian Revolution began in February 1917 with nearly spontaneous demonstrations to commemorate International Working Women's Day. These spread dramatically in just a few days, until the capital of Petrograd was paralyzed and the tsar toppled.

Far from a coup, the revolution depended on mass action—on thousands of confrontations like the one described by Trotsky in his *History of the Russian Revolution* between a crowd of workers and the Cossacks, the most brutal and feared unit of the tsar's army:

> The workers at the Erikson, one of the foremost mills in the Vyborg district, after a morning meeting, came out on the Sampsonievsky Prospect, a whole mass, 2,500 of them, and in a narrow place ran into the Cossacks. Cutting their way with the breasts of their horses, the officers first charged

> through the crowd. Behind them, filling the whole width of the Prospect, galloped the Cossacks. Decisive moment! But the horsemen, cautiously, in a long ribbon, rode through the corridor just made by the officers. "Some of them smiled," Kayurov recalls, "and one of them gave the workers a good wink." This wink was not without meaning. The workers were emboldened with a friendly, not hostile, kind of assurance, and slightly infected the Cossacks with it. The one who winked found imitators. In spite of renewed efforts from the officers, the Cossacks, without openly breaking discipline, failed to force the crowd to disperse, but flowed through it in streams. This was repeated three or four times and brought the two sides even closer together. Individual Cossacks began to reply to the workers' questions and even to enter into momentary conversations with them. Of discipline, there remained but a thin transparent shell that threatened to break through any second. The officers hastened to separate their patrol from the workers, and, abandoning the idea of dispersing them, lined the Cossacks out across the street as a barrier to prevent the demonstrators from getting to the [center of the city]. But even this did not help: Standing stock-still in perfect discipline, the Cossacks did not hinder the workers from "diving" under their horses. The revolution does not choose its paths: it made its first steps toward victory under the belly of a Cossack's horse.

If Lenin and Trotsky and the Bolshevik Party they led ended up as leaders of the new workers' state, it was because they earned that position. The Bolsheviks eventually became a majority of the representatives to the soviets, the workers' councils. At the time, no one with any knowledge of the situation questioned this mass support. As Martov, a prominent opponent of the Bolsheviks, wrote, "Understand, please, what we have before us after all is a victorious uprising of the proletariat—almost the entire proletariat supports Lenin and expects its social liberation from the uprising."

Even the final act of the revolution—the armed insurrection in October, in which workers took power from the capitalist government left behind after the tsar—was carried out with a minimum of resistance and violence.

The popular character of the Russian Revolution is also clear from looking at its initial accomplishments.

The revolution put an end to Russia's participation in the First World War—the terrible carnage that left millions of workers slaughtered in a conflict over which major powers would dominate the globe. Russia's entry into the war had been accompanied by a wave of patriotic frenzy, but masses of Russians came to reject the slaughter. The soldiers that the tsar depended on to defend his rule changed sides and joined the revolution—a decisive step in Russia, as it has been in all revolutions.

The Russian Revolution also dismantled the tsar's empire—what Lenin called a "prison-house" of different nations that suffered for years under tsarist tyranny. These nations were given the unconditional right to self-determination. The tsar had used the most vicious anti-Semitism to prop up his rule—after the revolution, Jews led the workers' councils in Russia's two biggest cities. Laws outlawing homosexuality were repealed. Abortion was legalized and made available on demand. And the revolution started to remove the age-old burden of "women's work" in the family by organizing socialized child care and communal kitchens and laundries.

But just listing the proclamations doesn't do justice to the reality of workers' power. Russia was a society in the process of being remade from the bottom up. In the factories, workers began to take charge of production. The country's vast peasantry took over the land of the big landowners. In city neighborhoods, people organized all sorts of communal services.

In general, decisions about the whole of society became decisions that the whole of society played a part in making. Russia became a cauldron of discussion—where the ideas of all were part of a debate about what to do. The memories of socialists who lived through the revolution are dominated by this sense of people's horizons opening up. As Krupskaya, a veteran of the Bolshevik Party and Lenin's wife, described it:

> I drank in the life around me. The streets in those days presented a curious spectacle: everywhere people stood about in knots, arguing heatedly and discussing the latest events. I used to mingle with the crowd and listen. These street meetings were so interesting that it once took me three hours to walk from Shirokaya Street to the Krzesinska Mansion. The house in which we lived overlooked a courtyard, and even here, if you opened the window at night, you could hear a heated dispute. A soldier would be sitting there, and he always had an audience—usually some of the cooks or housemaids from next door, or some young people. An hour after midnight, you could catch snatches of talk—"Bolsheviks, Mensheviks..." At three in the morning, "Milyukov, Bolsheviks..." At five—still the same street-corner-meeting talk, politics, etc. Petrograd's white nights are always associated in my mind now with those all-night political disputes.

The tragedy is that workers' power survived for only a short time in Russia. In the years that followed 1917, the world's major powers, including the United States, organized an invasion force that fought alongside the dregs of tsarist society—ex-generals, aristocrats, and assorted hangers-on—in a civil war against the new workers' state. The revolution survived this assault, but at a terrible price. By 1922, as a result of the civil war, famine stalked Russia. The working class—the class that had made the Russian Revolution—was decimated.

Neither Lenin nor any other leader of the Russian Revolution had any illusion that a workers' state could survive this barbarism without the support of revolutions in more advanced countries. The Russian revolutionaries believed that socialism could be started in Russia—but that it could only be finished after an international socialist revolution.

In fact, a wave of upheavals did sweep across Europe following the Russian Revolution and the end of the First World War, toppling monarchies in Germany and the Austro-Hungarian empire and shaking societies around the globe. But workers didn't succeed in taking power anywhere else for any length of time. So the Russian Revolution was left isolated.

In these desperate circumstances, Russia's shattered working class couldn't continue to exercise power through workers' councils. More and more, decisions were made by a group of state bureaucrats, led by Joseph Stalin. At first, the aim was to keep Russia's workers' state alive until help came in the form of international revolution. But eventually, as the hope of revolutions abroad faded, Stalin and his allies began to eliminate any and all opposition to their rule—and started making decisions on the basis of how best to protect and increase their own power. Though continuing to use the rhetoric of socialism, they began to take back every gain won in the revolution—without exception. The soviets became rubber stamps for the decisions of the regime. The tsar's empire was rebuilt. Women lost their newfound rights.

This counterrevolution wasn't carried out without opposition. In particular, Leon Trotsky led the struggle to defend socialist principles. To finally consolidate power, Stalin had to murder or hound into exile every single surviving leader of the 1917 revolution.

Russia under Stalin became the opposite of the workers' state of 1917. Though they mouthed socialist phrases, Stalin and the thugs who followed him ran a dictatorship where workers were every bit as exploited as in Western-style capitalist countries. They presided over a system of state capitalism—controlling society through state control over the economy.

Sadly, many people associate socialism with Stalin's tyranny—or with the top-down, undemocratic systems in China, Cuba, and other so-called "socialist" countries modeled on the old USSR. That's certainly what supporters of capitalism encourage us to believe. After all, what better argument could there be against socialism than the idea that any attempt to win change is doomed to produce another Stalin? But Stalin's triumph in Russia wasn't inevitable. It was the result of a workers' revolution left isolated in a sea of capitalism—strangled until it was finally defeated.

But none of this can erase what was accomplished by the revolution in Russia—the most backward society in Europe.

We're in a far better position today—something made plain by the examples of workers' struggles since 1917. The history of the twentieth century is filled with huge social explosions in which the struggles of workers took center stage. From France and Portugal in Europe, to Iran in the Middle East, to Chile in South America, to Poland under the thumb of the former Stalinist dictatorship in Eastern Europe, these upheavals—along with dozens of others—showed the power of workers to challenge the status quo and pose an alternative.

Though they failed to establish socialism, these revolutionary upheavals brought the mass of the population to life. And that is what socialism is about—a society created by the vast majority and organized around what they want it to be. As the British author of children's books Arthur Ransome wrote of the new world he witnessed in revolutionary Russia:

> We have seen the flight of the young eagles. Nothing can destroy that fact, even if, later in the day, the eagles fall to earth one by one, with broken wings.... These men who have made the Soviet government in Russia, if they must fail, will fail with clean shields and clean hearts, having striven for an ideal which will live beyond them. Even if they fail, they will nonetheless have written a page of history more daring than any other which I can remember in the history of humanity.

CHAPTER SEVEN

Why You Should Be a Socialist

If anyone is still wondering whether the U.S. invasion of Iraq was about oil, they should take a closer look at Executive Order 13303.

In May 2003, two months into the invasion, George Bush signed an order that essentially grants total immunity to U.S. oil companies operating in Iraq. So long as they can prove that their activities are related in some way to the extraction or transportation of oil pumped out of Iraq, the corporate giants have a get-out-of-jail-free card for any financial rip-off, human rights violation, or environmental damage that they commit—anywhere in the world. "As written, the executive order appears to cancel the rule of law for the oil industry," Tom Devine, legal director for the Government Accountability Project, told the *Los Angeles Times.*

With the ties between the exploitation of Iraq's oil wealth and the expansion of U.S. military power so obvious, it's little wonder that terms like "colonial" and "imperialism"—once dismissed as out-of-date left-wing rhetoric—are back in fashion. "Given the historical baggage that 'imperialism' carries, there's no need for the U.S. government to embrace the term," wrote one Washington hawk, the aptly named Max Boot. "But it should definitely embrace the practice."

Likewise, the intimate connections between the U.S. government's wars abroad and its class war waged on working people at home are plain to see. For example, not long after Bush installed him in the newly created position of Homeland Security tsar, Tom Ridge personally intervened to threaten the International Longshore and Warehouse Union (ILWU) with military scabs if workers on the West Coast docks took action to win a fair contract. The reason: A dock strike would be a "threat" to national security during the "war on terror."

Further evidence: Stevedoring Services of America was the leader of the hard-line shipping corporations when Ridge issued his threat. The company made the news again in early 2003—not long after the ILWU settled for an inferior contract—by using its White House connections to nab a contract for the "reconstruction" of Iraq, running the main Iraqi port of Umm Qasr.

All this illustrates the interconnectedness of corporate, political, and military power in the United States. But if there's any doubt, the best example of all is Bush's superhawk defense secretary, Donald Rumsfeld. Rumsfeld hasn't held an elected office since the 1960s, but he has exercised vast powers ever since—as a top appointee in Republican administrations, a job-slashing corporate executive in the private sector, and an important planner of U.S. military policy, whether he was part of official Washington or not.

If you ever wanted to understand what socialists mean when they talk about a capitalist ruling class that controls the resources of society and uses them to promote its own power and wealth, Donald Rumsfeld is a good place to start.

The great novelist and essayist James Baldwin could have had Rumsfeld in mind when he wrote:

> The civilized have created the wretched, quite coldly and deliberately, and do not intend to change the status quo; are responsible for their slaughter and enslavement; rain down bombs on defenseless children whenever and where they decide that their "vital interests" are menaced; and think nothing of torturing a man to death: these people are not to be taken seriously when they speak of the "sanctity" of human life, or the "conscience" of the civilized world.

Poverty and inequality, wars and violence—these aren't unfortunate mistakes or accidents in the modern world. The capitalist system is organized to produce them—"quite coldly and deliberately."

The stakes are higher than ever today—because America's rulers are intent on more wars around the globe, not fewer. They want more wealth, not less. They are intent on defending their power and privileges from any challenge around the world, but also at home—and they don't care about the cost that ordinary people pay.

At times, their power may seem too great to be challenged. But it should be remembered that African Americans feared the same about the murderous racists who ruled over the U.S. South during the era of Jim Crow segregation. The people of Eastern Europe believed that the tyrants who oppressed them were too powerful to be stopped. So did Blacks under South Africa's apartheid system. So has every victim of history's oppressors.

In today's America, we don't see the level of intensive and

widespread struggle associated with these world-changing movements. But we don't see submission and surrender either. The corporate media myth that ordinary people in U.S. society are content with their lives and with the society around them is false.

Thus, in spite of all the media cheerleading and the relentless propaganda offensive of the Bush White House, the drive to invade Iraq in 2003 stirred an unprecedented international antiwar movement. On February 15, before the war began, some ten million people took to the streets around the globe for a magnificent day of protests that shredded the U.S. government's hopes that it would be able to claim international support for its war.

Within the United States itself, antiwar protests and actions drew out far greater numbers than anything since the height of the struggle against the Vietnam War. The critics of the antiwar movement who claimed that activists were "too radical" turned out to be the ones who were "out of touch." As one protester, who traveled from North Carolina to Washington, D.C., for an antiwar march in January, told *Socialist Worker* newspaper: "This war has touched a nerve. We have a Gulf War veteran who came out in our bus, we have union delegates, we have people from the civil rights movement, people from the Unitarian church, Quakers—it's a slice of America."

Before this antiwar movement came the rise of an international global justice struggle that challenged the media celebration of the 1990s "miracle economy." The movement grabbed the spotlight suddenly at the end of 1999, when protests exploded during the World Trade Organization (WTO) conference in Seattle. Even the mainstream media had to notice that growing numbers of people weren't buying their happy talk. "They are folks who don't check each day to see how their 401(k) is doing or hang out with people who have become millionaires when their companies went public," the *Washington Post* reported. "What they all seem to agree on is that giant corporations have gone too far in gaining control over their lives and defining the values of their culture and that the WTO has become a handmaiden to those corporate interests."

Meanwhile, in countries around the world, there are signs of a rising class struggle—for example, in Latin America, where huge explosions of protest and anger have shaken Bolivia, Argentina, Ecuador, Venezuela, and beyond.

The spirit of all these struggles—the general strikes and street confrontations in South America, more modest grassroots organizing in the United States against sweatshops and economic injustice, the fight against Washington's war on the world—has given a new depth to the global justice movement. This political development has been on display at the World Social Forums—conferences that each year since 2001 have brought together tens of thousands of representatives of unions, social movements, and left-wing organizations. The forums have given expression to the growing resistance to a world of corporate greed and war with the slogan: Another world is possible.

And these are just the highlights. Often, the political activities that have taken place in recent years—demonstrations, strikes, boycotts, and petitioning—have gone unnoticed. Many protests were small. They didn't involve people beyond those personally connected to a particular issue, and therefore others who might have participated never heard of them.

In a system based on inequality and injustice, there are issues in every corner of society that spark outrage and need to bc organized around. But whether there is action—whether the protests get called, whether the petitions are circulated, whether the transportation is organized, and the signs get made—depends on what people decide to do.

This is where politics matter. No matter what issues they involve, struggles in the U.S. today all come in the wake of more than two decades of defeats for organizations of working people. This has had an impact on how people organize themselves to fight—even whether they fight.

The labor movement, for example, has been hammered by employer attacks that have pushed down the proportion of union workers to a low of 13 percent. In the face of this offensive, union leaders have come to argue that strikes and militant action are methods of the past that do more harm than good. Instead, they've devoted their resources to winning favor in Washington.

But while labor leaders have done their best to avoid a fight, in other cases, rank-and-file union members recognized that the stakes were too high *not* to take action. Often, these struggles involved people who aren't thought of as the core of the labor movement—sanitation workers, janitors, university clerical staff, and grocery workers, to name a few examples from 2003. But their willingness to take action sets a competing example for the labor movement.

So who's right? Are strikes outdated? Do militant tactics alienate our allies? Will the Democrats serve our interests? What strategies can help us win? These are political questions that have to be answered. And how they get answered will shape the struggles of the future.

In this sense, politics don't just belong to the politicians and the media commentators, or to union leaders and the heads of civil rights and liberal organizations. Politics belong to all of us—because how we answer political questions helps to decide what happens in society.

A revolutionary socialist party

Ideas can change very quickly in struggle. By taking action for even limited demands, people learn—or at least begin to learn—who their allies are, what they're up against, what works and what doesn't work in advancing their cause.

But ideas don't change all at once. There are always some groups of workers who, on the basis of greater experience and more extensive political discussions, are more determined to confront the bosses, more committed to standing up for the oppressed, more confident about fighting for a political alternative. Nor is the process static. People's consciousness changes under the impact of real events—victories and defeats in struggle, the overall political climate, and so on—going both forward and backward, and sometimes, in both directions at once.

The point is that at every step of the way, there are different ideas about what to do about any political issue. Some people will see the need to take action, to use more militant tactics, to make the link to other political issues. Others will argue that militant action makes matters worse. The outcome of these debates shapes the outcome of the struggle.

This is where the intervention of socialists—who can express the experience of past struggles and suggest a way forward—is crucial. An organization of socialists can unite people so that they can share their experiences and hammer out an understanding of how to fight back from day to day—in a workplace or community or school. The strength of such an organization is in the range of experiences and the political understanding of all its members.

None of this would be much use to a political party like the Democrats. The Democratic Party exists for one reason—to get Democrats elected to office. For that, it needs its supporters to vote once or twice every couple years.

Socialists have very different goals—so our political party will have to look very different. We need socialists in every workplace to agitate around fightbacks on the shop floor. We need socialists in every neighborhood to take up the questions of housing and police violence and health care. We need students to agitate on college campuses. We need socialists in every corner of society inhabited by working people, and we need these socialists working nonstop, organizing struggle and carrying on political discussions.

This commitment to struggle is part of our socialist tradition. Socialists have always been at the forefront of the fight for a better world—leaders in the union movement, in the movement against racism, in the fight against war, and many other struggles.

To achieve its aims, a revolutionary socialist organization has to be more democratic than other political organizations under capitalism. We need to bring together the experiences of every socialist—and to make those experiences part of the common basis that we all organize on.

But a socialist organization has to be centralized—to be prepared to act together in the fight against the bosses. Why the need for a centralized organization? Because the other side is organized. The basis of their power is the profit they make at the workplace—highly organized systems built around exploiting workers. Their side organizes political propaganda through the media. Their side responds to resistance with a highly organized and disciplined police force and army.

We need an organization for our side—one that can coordinate actions not just in one workplace or even one city, but around the country. We need an organization that can put forward a common set of ideas—using its own newspapers and magazines and books. Socialists have to be able to fight around the same program, whether they're teachers or autoworkers or college students, and whether they live in Chicago or New York or Los Angeles—and ultimately in Seoul or London or Johannesburg.

The bigger the struggle, the more complex and urgent the political questions. In the Russian Revolution of 1917, the hated tsar was toppled in a matter of a few days. That part of the revolution was almost completely spontaneous. No socialist organization picked the date for the demonstrations that snowballed into a mass movement. The accumulated hatred for the tsar and his regime was all that was necessary.

But the issue of what came next raised questions that couldn't be answered with spontaneous action. Within the governments that came to power after the tsar were people who called themselves socialists—and who claimed that the revolution had to be demobilized for the people's victories to be consolidated. Were they right? What should be done to make sure that the tsar never came to power again? How could democracy and justice be spread even further?

These questions were hotly debated throughout Russian society. The reason that they were ultimately given socialist answers is because a tried-and-tested revolutionary socialist organization existed to make its case. On the basis of its past experience and its roots among workers across Russia, the Bolshevik Party was able to recognize and make sense of the situation in all its complexity—and to express the aims of socialism that workers favored.

This didn't happen overnight. Lenin and his Bolsheviks worked for a period of years, under very difficult conditions, to build their influence into as many corners of the working-class movement as possible. Their goal was that all Bolsheviks, not just the party's leaders, would be viewed by people they worked with as committed and battle-hardened activists with a real alternative to offer.

With this goal at its heart, a revolutionary party can be completely flexible in terms of tactics, but rock-hard in its principles. In a conservative period, it can preserve revolutionary traditions from attempts to destroy them or water them down. In a radicalizing period, it can make its case for how the movement can go forward, based on its members' understanding of the lessons of the past and their own experiences in the struggles of the present.

Sadly, the need for socialist organization has been proven many times since 1917—but in the negative. Too many times, mass mobilizations of workers threw the status quo into question—only to allow it back in because socialists weren't in a position to make the case for how to go forward.

This, then, is the further case for why you should be a socialist—not just in thought, but in deed, as a member of a socialist organization. As individuals on our own, we can't accomplish much—not even with the best grasp of what's wrong with the world and how it could be different. But as part of an organization, we can make a difference.

This isn't an abstract question. There are towns in the Midwest where Ku Klux Klan members no longer parade around because socialists took the initiative to confront them. There are former death-row prisoners who are alive today because socialists, along with others, drew attention to their cases and showed why they shouldn't be executed. There are workplaces where supervisors can't get away with whatever they want because socialists stood up to them.

Socialists can and do make a difference right now. We need to make more of a difference. We need socialists in every workplace, on every campus, in every neighborhood—involved in every struggle throughout society.

But there's a further task. Socialists need to show how the day-to-day fights of today are part of a long-term fight for bigger political changes. As Marx and Engels put it more than a 150 years ago: "The Communists fight for the attainment of the immediate aims, for the enforcement of the momentary interests of the working class; but in the movement of the present, they also represent and take care of the future of that movement."

Socialists are among the best fighters in the struggles of today, but we're also involved in the struggle for the future—ultimately, for a different kind of society where exploitation and oppression are never known again.

We live in a rotten and barbaric world—a world of poverty, famines, environmental degradation, and bloody wars. For huge numbers of people, just surviving from day to day is intolerably difficult. For the rest of the vast majority, the struggle to get by leaves almost no time for leisure—much less for putting our minds to making the world a better place to live.

To hear defenders of the system explain it, this is inevitable. It may not be a perfect world, we're told, but it's the best we can do—and the best we can hope for is to stop it from getting worse.

What a sick society it is that tells us that six million children dead of malnutrition each year is the best we can do. That the suffering and carnage in Iraq and countries around the globe is the best we can do. That a world threatened by ecological disaster is the best we can do.

We don't have to pay that price. The resources exist to eliminate these horrors—and build a socialist society free of poverty and oppression, where we all have control over our lives.

That is a world worth fighting for.

AFTERWORD BY HOWARD ZINN

Eugene V. Debs and the Idea of Socialism

We are always in need of radicals who are also lovable, and so we would do well to remember Eugene Victor Debs. Ninety years ago, and the time the *Progressive* was born, Debs was nationally famous as leader of the Socialist Party, and the poet James Whitcomb Riley wrote of him:

> As warm a heart as ever beat
> Betwixt here and the Judgment Seat.

Debs was what every socialist or anarchist or radical should be: fierce in his convictions, kind and compassionate in his personal relations. Sam Moore, a fellow inmate of the Atlanta penitentiary, where Debs was imprisoned for opposing the First World War, remembered how he felt as Debs was about to be released on Christmas Day, 1921:

> As miserable as I was, I would defy fate with all its cruelty as long as Debs held my hand, and I was the most miserably happiest man on Earth when I knew he was going home Christmas.

Howard Zinn is author of *A People's History of the United States*. This article first appeared in the January 1999 *Progressive*, and is reprinted here with permission from both the author and the magazine.

Debs had won the hearts of his fellow prisoners in Atlanta. He had fought for them in a hundred ways and refused any special privileges for himself. On the day of his release, the warden ignored prison regulations and opened every cellblock to allow more than 2,000 inmates to gather in front of the main jail building to say goodbye to Eugene Debs. As he started down the walkway from the prison, a roar went up and he turned, tears streaming down his face, and stretched out his arms to the other prisoners.

This was not his first prison experience. In 1894, not yet a socialist but an organizer for the American Railway Union, he had led a nationwide boycott of the railroads in support of the striking workers at the Pullman Palace Car Company. They tied up the railroad system, burned hundreds of railway cars, and were met with the full force of the capitalist state: Attorney General Richard Olney, a former railroad lawyer, got a court injunction to prohibit blocking trains. President Cleveland called out the army, which used bayonets and rifle fire on a crowd of 5,000 strike sympathizers in Chicago. Seven hundred were arrested. Thirteen were shot to death.

Debs was jailed for violating an injunction prohibiting him from doing or saying anything to carry on the strike. In court, he denied he was a socialist, but during his six months in prison he read socialist literature, and the events of the strike took on a deeper meaning. He wrote later:

> I was to be baptized in socialism in the roar of conflict. In the gleam of every bayonet and the flash of every rifle the class struggle was revealed.

From then on, Debs devoted his life to the cause of working people and the dream of a socialist society. He stood on the platform with Mother Jones and Big Bill Haywood in 1905 at the founding convention of the Industrial Workers of the World. He was a magnificent speaker, his long body leaning forward from the podium, his arm raised dramatically. Thousands came to hear him talk all over the country.

With the outbreak of war in Europe in 1914 and the buildup of war fever against Germany, some socialists succumbed to the talk of "preparedness," but Debs was adamantly opposed. When President Wilson and Congress brought the nation into the war in 1917, speech was no longer free. The Espionage Act made it a crime to say anything that would discourage enlistment in the armed forces.

Soon, close to 1,000 people were in prison for protesting the war. The producer of a movie called *The Spirit of '76*, about the American revolution, was sentenced to ten years in prison for promoting anti-British feeling at a time when England and the United States were allies. The case was officially labeled *The U.S. v. The Spirit of '76*.

Debs made a speech in Canton, Ohio, in support of the men and women in jail for opposing the war. He told his listeners:

> Wars throughout history have been waged for conquest and plunder. And that is war, in a nutshell. The master class has always declared the wars; the subject class has always fought the battles.

He was found guilty and sentenced to ten years in prison by a judge who denounced those "who would strike the sword from the hand of the nation while she is engaged in defending herself against a foreign and brutal power."

In court, Debs refused to call any witnesses, declaring: "I have been accused of obstructing the war. I admit it. I abhor war. I would oppose war if I stood alone." Before sentencing, Debs spoke to judge and jury, uttering perhaps his most famous words. I was in his hometown of Terre Haute, Indiana, recently, among 200 people gathered to honor his memory, and we began the evening by reciting those words—words that moved me deeply when I first read them and move me deeply still:

> While there is a lower class, I am in it. While there is a criminal element, I am of it. While there is a soul in prison, I am not free.

The "liberal" Oliver Wendell Holmes, speaking for a unanimous Supreme Court, upheld the verdict, on the ground that Debs's speech was intended to obstruct military recruiting. When the war as over, the "liberal" Woodrow Wilson turned down his Attorney General's recommendation that Debs be released, even though he was sixty-five and in poor health. Debs was in prison for thirty-two months. Finally, in 1921, the Republican Warren Harding ordered him freed on Christmas Day.

Today, when capitalism, "the free market," and "private enterprise" are being hailed as triumphant in the world, it is a good time to remember Debs and to rekindle the idea of socialism.

To see the disintegration of the Soviet Union as a sign of the failure of socialism is to mistake the monstrous tyranny created by Stalin for the vision of an egalitarian and democratic society that has inspired enormous numbers of people all over the world. Indeed, the removal of the Soviet Union as the false surrogate for the idea of socialism creates a great opportunity. We can now reintroduce genuine socialism to a world feeling the sickness of capitalism—its nationalist hatreds, its perpetual warfare, riches for a small number of people in a small number of countries, and hunger, homelessness, insecurity for everyone else.

Here in the United States we should recall that enthusiasm for socialism—production for use instead of profit, economic and social equality, solidarity with our brothers and sisters all over the world—was at its height before the Soviet Union came into being.

In the era of Debs, the first seventeen years of the twentieth century—until war created an opportunity to crush the movement—millions of Americans declared their adherence to the principles of socialism. Those were years of bitter labor struggles, the great walkouts of women garment workers in New York, the victorious multi-ethnic strike of textile workers in Lawrence, Massachusetts, the unbelievable courage of coal miners in Colorado, defying the power and wealth of the Rockefellers. The I.W.W. was born—revolutionary, militant, demanding "one big union" for everyone, skilled and unskilled, black and white, men and women, native-born and foreign-born.

More than a million people read *Appeal to Reason* and other socialist newspapers. In proportion to population, it would be as if today more than three million Americans read a socialist press. The party had 100,000 members, and 1,200 office-holders in 340 municipalities. Socialism was especially strong in the Southwest, among tenant farmers, railroad workers, coal miners, lumberjacks. Oklahoma had 12,000 dues-paying members in 1914 and more than 100 socialists in local offices. It was the home of the fiery Kate Richards

O'Hare. Jailed for opposing the war, she once hurled a book through the skylight to bring fresh air into the foul-smelling jail block, bringing cheers from her fellow inmates.

The point of recalling all this is to remind us of the powerful appeal of the socialist idea to people alienated from the political system and aware of the growing stark disparities in income and wealth—as so many Americans are today. The word itself—"socialism"—may still carry the distortions of recent experience in bad places usurping the name. But anyone who goes around the country, or reads carefully the public opinion surveys over the past decade, can see that huge numbers of Americans agree on what should be the fundamental elements of a decent society: guaranteed food, housing, medical care for everyone; bread and butter as better guarantees of "national security" than guns and bombs; democratic control of corporate power; equal rights for all races, genders, and sexual orientations; a recognition of the rights of immigrants as the unrecognized counterparts of our parents and grandparents; the rejection of war and violence as solutions for tyranny and injustice.

There are people fearful of the word, all along the political spectrum. What is important, I think, is not the word, but a determination to hold up before a troubled public those ideas that are both bold and inviting—the more bold, the more inviting. That's what remembering Debs and the socialist idea can do for us.

Further Reading

I think the most important reading material of all is *Socialist Worker* (www.socialistworker.org), the newspaper of the International Socialist Organization. *SW* comes out weekly, crammed to the bursting point with news, political analysis, stories about the history of our movement, and reports of struggle. Of course, I'm biased—since I've worked on *SW* for the past two decades. A lot of the information and ideas in this book have appeared in its pages (almost always written by someone other than me). I owe a great debt to the people who've written for *Socialist Worker* and devoted their enormous talents to producing it.

The *International Socialist Review* (www.isreview.org) was launched in 1997, but I think that it has already become the best left-wing journal around. The *ISR* comes out every two months, and it's an indispensable source for political discussion and debate, involving a wide and growing list of contributors. I turn to the *ISR* constantly, both for facts and perspectives about contemporary political issues and discussions of historical and theoretical questions.

Two of the best short introductory books on socialism that have helped me enormously are Paul Foot's *Why You Should Join the Socialists* and John Molyneux's *Arguments for Revolutionary Socialism.* Unfortunately, both are out of print, but stray copies can sometimes be found in used bookstores or borrowed from socialists who picked up a copy years ago.

As part of its new series, the International Socialist Tradition, Haymarket Books recently republished a valuable short book by John Molyneux called *What Is the Real Marxist Tradition?* which is especially good at explaining why working-class self-emancipation is at the heart of socialism. So is the excellent *Two Souls of Socialism,* by Hal Draper. Also available from Haymarket, this pamphlet compares the different brands of socialism with the principles that Karl Marx stood for. Another essential introductory book about socialism is by Chris Harman. *How Marxism Works* is a clear and concise account of the basic ideas of the Marxist tradition.

The best introduction to Marxism was written by Marx. The 150-year-old *Communist Manifesto* reads as if it only arrived from the printer last week. Likewise, Lenin's short book *Imperialism* should be the first stop for anyone wanting to know more about the drive to war under capitalism, and Rosa Luxemburg's *Reform or Revolution* makes the case as clearly as anyone ever has for why the system can't be fixed.

For the history of the rich tradition of struggle in America, *A People's History of the United States* by Howard Zinn is a great place to start. There are a number of histories of the U.S. labor movement—one of the best is *American Labor Struggles* by Samuel Yellen. Sidney Lens's *The Forging of the*

American Empire documents how the United States has conducted more than 160 wars and other military ventures, while claiming to love peace. A new book by Sharon Smith called *Women and Socialism* collects a number of articles that take up the question of women's oppression and social issues in the U.S. today. Among the great wealth of books on the struggle of African Americans, a couple must-reads are *The Autobiography of Malcolm X*, and *In Struggle: SNCC and the Black Awakening of the 1960s* by Clayborne Carson.

There's a lot to read about the Russian Revolution. Your first book should be *Ten Days That Shook the World,* an eyewitness account by the American journalist and socialist John Reed. Leon Trotsky's *History of the Russian Revolution* is more than 1,200 pages long, but every page is worth the read. Tony Cliff's multipart political biographies of *Lenin* and *Trotsky* are excellent guides to the ideas of these two revolutionary leaders and the events they participated in. And for understanding what happened to Russia after the revolution, check out *Russia: From Workers' State to State Capitalism.*

Most of these books and publications are available from Haymarket Books. Look for Haymarket's store on the Web at www.haymarketbooks.org. For further information on Haymarket, call 773-583-7884, e-mail orders@haymarketbooks.org, or write: Haymarket Books, P.O. Box 180165, Chicago, IL 60618.

About Haymarket Books

Haymarket Books is a non-profit, progressive book distributor and publisher, a project of the Center for Economic Research and Social Change.

We take inspiration and courage from our namesakes, the Haymarket Martyrs, who gave their lives fighting for a better world. Their struggle for the eight-hour day in 1886, which gave us May Day, the international workers' holiday, reminds workers around the world that ordinary people can organize and struggle for their own liberation.

It was August Spies, one of the Martyrs who was targeted for being an immigrant and an anarchist, who predicted the battles being fought to this day. "If you think that by hanging us you can stamp out the labor movement," Spies told the judge, "then hang us. Here you will tread upon a spark, but here, and there, and behind you, and in front of you, and everywhere, the flames will blaze up. It is a subterranean fire. You cannot put it out. The ground is on fire upon which you stand."

Also from Haymarket Books

The Struggle for Palestine

Edited by Lance Selfa ISBN 1931859000 2002

In this important new collection of essays, leading international solidarity activists offer insight into the ongoing struggle for Palestinian freedom and for justice in the Middle East.

The Forging of the American Empire

By Sidney Lens ISBN 0745321003 2003

This is the story of a nation—the United States—that has conducted more than 160 wars and other military ventures while insisting that it loves peace. In the process, the U.S. has forged a world empire while maintaining its innocence of imperialistic designs.

Trotsky's Marxism and Other Essays

By Duncan Hallas ISBN 1931859035 2003

No serious attempt to understand the tragedy of the Russian Revolution—and its relevance to the building of socialism today—can ignore the unique contribution made by Leon Trotsky. Leon Trotsky was one of the major architects of the October Revolution of 1917 and an organizer of the Red Army. Ironically, it also fell to him to chronicle and analyze the degeneration and destruction of socialism in Russia under Stalin's regime.